GROWING OLDER GRACEFULLY

31 REFLECTIONS ON FINISHING WELL

ENDORSEMENTS

In almost two decades of ministering to seniors, I have witnessed the joys and challenges the sunset years can bring. Our journey is infused with hope when we invite Jesus to help us finish well. *Growing Older Gracefully* offers a wonderful, daily map to help seniors finish their race strong and fruitful as they renew their trust and hope in Jesus Christ. This book will be a treasure and deep blessing to any believer who desires to finish their life strong and to glorify their Savior.

—Mark E. Eggleston, Spiritual Care Administrator and Chaplain, Western Home Communities

"Old age ain't no place for sissies," said Betty Davis, as quoted in this volume. At the same time, old age is a gift from God, Pastor Dave Claassen reminds us throughout *Growing Older Gracefully*. This devotional addresses the realities of growing older from a glass half full perspective. As Pastor Claassen puts it, "Spiritually, our senior years can be the most fruitful years of our life." Senior citizens will be inspired to use their time and life experience wisely, being grateful for each moment and finding new opportunities to bless others, from grandchildren to neighbors to caregivers.

—David Yonke, author and retired journalist

Although I am not a big book reader, David Claassen's *Growing Older Gracefully* was an easy read. I did learn from this that I do not want to be that Old Grump. As I face retirement in a few years, I plan to read this book again in a year and again in a couple years after that as I continue to work at *Growing Older Gracefully*.

—**Bill Beutin**, editor of the *Golden View Newspaper*, dedicated to the young at heart.

With themes of gratitude, calling, and contentment, David Claassen shares many ideas about finishing life well. His suggestion to read one chapter daily for thirty-one days is a wonderful way to keep the thoughts alive. Since I am a hugger, I loved the idea of intentionally embracing the moment and "hugging" the hour and making the most of opportunities that God gives us each day. The book is easy reading but has depth and substance to reflect on, and I found it very encouraging. If God gave us this privilege of older living, he has us here for a purpose. Grumbling or gratitude is a choice. I recommend this for the senior grumps in your life! They may replace their grumbling with gratitude and grace.

—**Carol Wilson**, director of KeenAgers, Coral Ridge Presbyterian Church

Whether you're embarking on your own journey of aging or supporting a loved one through theirs, *Growing Older Gracefully* offers invaluable insights and a gentle reminder that with each passing year comes an opportunity for growth, resilience, and wisdom. With a blend of practical wisdom and charming anecdotes, this book serves as a beacon of light for those navigating the journey of growing older.

—**Rev. Rupert Loyd Jr.**, PhD, lead pastor Marketplace Community Church

Just three pages into the manuscript I knew I couldn't wait for the book to be published. At this time, I am early in the fifth year of my retirement, but I can already see from Dave's statements how I have been allowing myself to succumb to some of the typical behavior patterns so many of us slide into as we enter our Golden Years. I'm just hoping I can be a better Rudy as I advance through my years. Personally, I can't think of a single time in the years I interacted with Dave that he didn't look joyful. But that's just one of the many insights, or pearls of wisdom, that awaits you. I look forward to sharing this book with family and friends. As one of the younger members of my family, I pray many of them can still benefit from Dave's insights and wisdom.
—**Alan Cox**, twenty-eight-year employee City of Toledo, Ohio; ten-year union president American Federation of State, County, and Municipal Employees (AFSCME)

GROWING OLDER GRACEFULLY

31 REFLECTIONS ON FINISHING WELL

DAVID J. CLAASSEN

ELK LAKE PUBLISHING INC®

PUBLISHING THE POSITIVE
Plymouth, Massachusetts

A Christian Company
ElkLakePublishingInc.com

COPYRIGHT NOTICE

Cover and Interior Design: Kelly Artieri, Deb Haggerty
Editor(s): Peggy Ellis, Judy Hagey, Deb Haggerty

PUBLISHED BY: Elk Lake Publishing, Inc., 35 Dogwood Drive, Plymouth, MA 02360, 2024

Library Cataloging Data
Names: Claassen, David J. (David J. Claassen)
Growing Older Gracefully: 31 Reflections on Finishing Well / David Claassen
154p. 23cm × 15cm (9in × 6 in.)
154ISBN-13: 9798891341890 (paperback) | 9798891341906 (trade paperback) | 9798891341913 (e-book)
Key Words: older; aging; aged; geriatric; senior; retired; retirement
Library of Congress Control Number: 2024939503 Nonfiction

DEDICATION

For our parents, John and Clara Claassen and Dick and Pauline Blom, who taught and modeled how to grow older gracefully and finish well.

TABLE OF CONTENTS

ACKNOWLEDGMENTS

No book is a solo project. I'm greatly indebted to my wife, Diann, who has always been a partner with me in my writing, including this project. I also am grateful for Peggy Ellis, Judy Hagey, and Deb Haggerty, my editors at Elk Lake Publishing, for their expertise in helping me take my writing to the next level.

INTRODUCTION

I suspect we have a lot in common. Since you're reading this, chances are you're in the senior years or fast approaching them. I've been a senior for a surprising number of years. So, here we are in this unique stage of life. True, the circumstances for every age group are unique, and so are the golden years. We can use all the help we can get navigating the senior years. This is why I'm inviting you to join me on a thirty-one-day journey exploring what it means to grow older gracefully.

Let's journey slowly. We can be tempted to breeze through more than one day's reading at a time. After all, the readings aren't long. We're old enough to remember the speed-reading craze from a few decades ago where we were taught how to read much material fast. I wrote slowly, so I hope you read slowly. Let's take our time reflecting on each day's reading on finishing well.

You'll see three recurring themes as we journey together: gratitude, calling, and contentment. This wasn't intentional—it just happened. In retrospect, I'm not surprised. These three concepts play crucial roles in finishing life well.

Now, let's get started on our month's journey together.
Enjoy!

GROWING OLDER,
NOT GRUMPIER—DAY 1

The sign along Highway 3 in Iowa identifying the nearby town of Readlyn states, READLYN 857 friendly PEOPLE & one old GRUMP. The legend has been part of the town's history for years concerning a hobo who got off the train and decided he would make Readlyn his home. The hobo's demeanor prompted people to call him "the Old Grump."

Now that I'm well into my senior years, I'm thinking more about that Old Grump of Readlyn, Iowa, and how I don't want to be like him. If we counted the people on my street, those in my church family, and my extended family, I don't want the tally coming up one person short with the addendum, "and one Old Grump," referring to me.

Grumpy people can be any age, but it seems the label is most often applied to the older population. As I continue my senior journey, I want the story of The Old Grump of Readlyn, Iowa, to inspire me not to be like him.

I've learned much from the examples of others on how to grow older gracefully and how not to. I spent almost forty years pastoring a church that contained many seniors. We always had fifteen or more on what we called our "shut-in" list, those folks who no longer drove, were homebound, or were living in an assisted living facility or nursing home. I visited these seniors hundreds of times. I sought to comfort and help them, acting as a spiritual adviser, but I often found they taught me and modeled for me, by both good example and bad example, how to grow older gracefully.

Jackie was one of our nursing home shut-ins who knew how to grow older gracefully. She had a wonderful, vivacious personality, always with a ready smile. Jackie got around the nursing home in a motorized wheelchair. While visiting Jackie, she shared how she had attached one end of a rope to a friend's wheelchair that was hand powered, the other end being attached to the back of her motorized wheelchair. She described, with a big grin, pulling her friend down the nursing home hallway. With the grin still in full force, she added the staff had reprimanded her for doing so, telling her she wasn't to do so again. As I grow older, I want to emulate Jackie and other senior citizens like her.

Growing older is *not* an option. We all grow older until we die, but *how* we grow older *is* an option. We make choices every day as to whether we will become an old grump or grow into a more gracious person. We might not always realize we're making such choices, but we are. Our inattentiveness to the process can result in our growing older in an ungracious way. We should be intentional about the aging process.

Growing older is a privilege not all are granted. Will we use the privilege wisely? Old age is a gift. Will we unpack the gift of these days with appreciation and a determination, making the best of them?

Part of my own way of preparing for growing older gracefully is collecting and crafting thoughts on the subject, then putting them on these pages. Over the years, I've found whatever subject I preach, teach, or write on for the benefit of others benefits me even more. My prayer is you gain something from our thirty-one-day journey together, but I'm already certain I will gain the most from our shared journey.

A second motivation for putting some thoughts down in a small book like this is the possibility that, if I drift toward being an old grump, my wife or our children will be quick to toss a copy of this book in my lap, telling me to read what I wrote. This motivates me to practice what I preach, or in this case, what I write.

Growing Older Gracefully is the title of this small book for good reasons. "Growing" is the first word. We can continue "growing" as we get older. More on this later. "Older" is the second word in the title. I chose the word "older" instead of "old" because we are not "old," which is a state of being. Growing "older" suggests a process, a journey. More on this later as well.

"Gracefully" is the last word in the title. Grace and its derivatives are such wonderful words. Yes, you guessed it, more on this wonderful word "grace" later as we journey these thirty-one days together. Gracefully is a sibling word to the word graceful, which, if you reverse its two parts, means being full of grace. Being full of grace means being pleasant, sweet (not a sourpuss), and attractive (not necessarily in looks, but in the sense that people are attracted to us). But, most importantly, it means extending undeserved favor to those around us.

The apostle Paul faced many grueling situations as he fulfilled the call of Christ for him as an apostle. His ministry took a toll on him. Considering all he went through, we can assume he aged at a rate more rapid than normal. In addressing the Christians in the city of Corinth, he penned these words, recorded for our benefit many years later. "Therefore we do not lose heart. Though outwardly we are wasting away, yet inwardly we are being renewed day by day" (2 Corinthians 4:16). My prayer is that over the next thirty-one days, we'll find ourselves "being renewed day by day."

Thanks for picking up this little book that, by God's grace, can be a travel guide for us as we reflect together on our journey of growing older. I believe this can be a fulfilling journey for us—despite the many challenges that come with the aging process—if we decide to make it so.

THE FEARS OF GETTING OLD—
DAY 2

Every stage of life has its own fears. Children might fear the bogeyman under the bed, school-aged children and teenagers often fear not being accepted, young adults might fear not finding a person who will marry them, middle-aged people often fear not being successful. We seniors also have our fears—a significant number relating to the aging process—loss of freedom, significance, and health, just to name three.

In my years of ministering to the elderly, I've observed they often seemed more fearful than those who are younger, more fearful than when they themselves were younger. Perhaps some increased fearfulness results from physiological changes in the brain over which we have no control. However, many fears that come with aging can be faced with the conviction we can gain some control over them. We'll deal with specific fears we're likely to face in the later years of life in future daily reflections during this thirty-one-day journey. For now, let's reflect on the general state of being fearful in our senior years. Growing older gracefully means facing those fears and doing something about them.

The good news is, as older human beings, we have accumulated many past experiences from which we can draw in our later years. After all, we've survived everything thus far, right? There were difficult times, even terrible times, and tragedies, but somehow here we are—survivors. God has been with us in the past, which can give us the confidence he will be with us now and on into our future. We can face our fears related to the aging process with our faith in God.

This faith we have in God differs for each person. For some of us, we've followed the Lord during a significant portion of our life. He's seen us through a lot. We can decide to believe he will see us through until the end. We have the history—the history of our faith in God—that can create and sustain the momentum which pushes us forward.

However, some people reading this might feel they haven't focused on God much at all in the years leading to the present. If this describes you, let me reassure you that, even though you might not have actively sought out God or determined to follow him and his will, he has been shadowing you all along, a silent, unseen, ever-present help. Today is not too late to give him credit for how he's been there for you in the past. He's a gracious, forgiving God. You don't need to have racked up a bunch of points to get his help now. Acknowledging in the present his unacknowledged presence and help in the past can put you on firm footing for facing the future without fear.

We can take a couple of simple steps, making certain we're right with the Lord—that we're in a right relationship with him. First, we must acknowledge our need for his forgiveness of our sins. He offers us this forgiveness. We only need to ask. He's already provided the way of forgiveness for us when he sent his son Jesus to earth, having him go to the cross and die for our sins. He did that for us. We need only receive his gift of forgiveness, accepting Jesus as our Savior.

Then, second, we commit to living the rest of our lives for him, with deep gratitude for his forgiveness and with great joy for now being in a relationship with him. This means letting him be Lord of our lives. Having him as Savior and Lord is what makes us right with God. Having this true faith in the Lord is what can help us deal with our fears.

I find great comfort and a good antidote to fear in the words the old psalmist penned. "I was young and now I am old, yet I have never seen the righteous forsaken or their children begging bread" (Psalm 37:25). Considering how God has worked in our lives in the past can build our confidence he will work with us concerning our present and future issues of aging.

We can draw upon both the bad and the good that has happened to us in the past while facing our present and our future. Past calamities or successes can both be foundation stones upon which we can build a strong faith for today and tomorrow.

Of all people, we who have more years behind us should have confidence the Lord still goes before us. God says, "Even to your old age and gray hairs I am he, I am he who will sustain you. I have made you and I will carry you; I will sustain you and I will rescue you" (Isaiah 46:4).

We who are older often have more free time, which we can use for deepening our relationship with God. If reading the Bible regularly has been a habit in the past, we should keep practicing the habit. If reading what God says in the Bible has not been a regular habit in the past, we can use some of the extra time in our retirement years delving into

His Word, establishing a new habit, a holy habit. Reading God's Word strengthens our faith in him. When our faith is strengthened, our fears decrease. An old Irish proverb says, "Fear knocked at the door, faith answered, no one was there" (Origin unknown).

Talking with God about our fears helps—even about our inability to trust him as we know we should. Again, if we've always had the daily habit of talking with God in what we call prayer, then we should keep the communication going. Now is a good time to start if praying has not been our regular habit.

The apostle Paul wrote, "Do not be anxious about anything, but in every situation, by prayer and petition, with thanksgiving, present your requests to God. And the peace of God, which transcends all understanding, will guard your hearts and your minds in Christ Jesus" (Philippians 4:6–7).

We face unique fears as we grow older. More than ever, we should remember that fears flee in the face of faith.

GROWING OLDER, LIKE A TREE—DAY 3

When a tree is cut down, the growth rings are exposed—a ring for every year the tree lived. Some growth rings are wide; those were good years when the tree had all the resources needed for thriving. Some growth rings are narrow; those were tough years for the tree with little growth. Nevertheless, they did grow. What's interesting is the tree has a growth ring for every year, including the year the tree died or was cut down. The growth rings are a silent message—trees never stop growing until they die. Neither should people.

Anna Mary Robertson Moses was interested in art even as a child, but she was unable to do much artistically for many years. She was a housekeeper starting at the age of twelve and was so employed for fifteen years. She married, farming alongside her husband. They had ten children, five dying in infancy, making for a busy and challenging life. Beginning at age seventy-eight, she gave painting her serious attention. This new career took off. She became famous as a painter, being better known as Grandma Moses.

Speaking of Moses, the original Moses, the one in the Bible, was eighty years old when God called him to lead the

Israelites out of Egyptian slavery. Then too, there were the two people who encountered the infant Jesus in the temple in Jerusalem when Joseph and Mary brought him for consecration before the Lord. They were the devout Simeon and the prophetess Anna, both very old. The apostle John wrote five books in our Bible—a gospel, three letters, and the book of Revelation. Without question, he wrote them when he was old. Most scholars believe he was very old when he penned Revelation. God loves working with old people.

Most everyone enjoys celebrating the achievements of older people. Around graduation time each year, there are profiles of people graduating from high school or college who are well advanced in years. The common theme in these stories is the enthusiastic celebration by family, friends, and fellow students young enough to be the celebrated graduate's grandchildren or great-grandchildren.

We love stories about older people who try something new or achieve a milestone later in life, whether they're stories in the Bible or outside the Bible. They can inspire our own continuing development as we grow older.

Parker Palmer writes, "We need to reframe aging as a passage of discovery and engagement, not decline and inaction."[1] This doesn't mean we adopt a bucket list that includes skydiving, going back to school, or running a marathon. There are countless ways we can continue developing, growing as a person, or exploring new ways for impacting those in our sphere of influence. God's call for each of us to grow older gracefully is a unique call.

As a young pastor, which was a long time ago, I admired the senior citizens in my church who enthusiastically participated in Bible studies. Now I'm the senior citizen, determined I should live out what they modeled for me so many years ago—learning and growing in my walk with the Lord.

Sometimes, I'm frustrated upon learning a new insight from the Bible, grumbling that I hadn't seen the insight years earlier. I must remind myself the fact I'm still discovering new things in the Bible is good, that God's Word is inexhaustible. We should continue being a student of God's Word until our final graduation day, the day when we die. What the apostle Paul wrote to the Thessalonian Christians, complimenting them, has application for us as well. "Your faith is growing more and more" (2 Thessalonians 1:3). As we grow older, our faith should grow more and more.

New opportunities for being God's person among those in our sphere of influence are still available as we grow older. "I've outlived all my friends" is a lament that need never come from our lips. We can work at nurturing relationships with people younger than we are.

We're mistaken when we believe those younger than us don't enjoy hanging around with old people. If we're an interesting person who is interested in them, they'll enjoy a relationship with someone much older.

Perhaps, though, despite our best efforts, our sphere of influence might shrink with retirement from work, decreasing mobility, or other factors. But the remaining relationships can grow deeper. The older we get the less likely we'll find ourselves in a rush, allowing for more quality time for the relationships we have. During the first part of Jesus's three-year ministry, he often addressed large crowds, but as time went on, he focused on his twelve disciples. Shifting our focus of influence toward those who most likely will attend our funeral or memorial service can be a natural and proper realignment of our priorities. Whatever the number, we can continue carrying out God's call on our life, blessing those he's put around us.

Just as a tree doesn't stop growing until it dies, so we, until we draw our last breath, should live with the conviction that God is not finished with us. We still have things to learn, work to do.

Let's embrace the following great promise from God: "The righteous will flourish like a palm tree, they will grow like a cedar of Lebanon; planted in the house of the Lord, they will flourish in the courts of our God. They will still bear fruit in old age, they will stay fresh and green" (Psalm 92:12–14).

We can continue growing in him and in our obedience to him. We can continue staying fresh and green.

LET FAITH KEEP YOU FLEXIBLE— DAY 4

"Old people are stuck in their ways" is often the assessment the younger generation makes concerning those who are older. In all honesty, it's also a frequent self-assessment of us older people. We do like our routines.

As a pastor, I often visited an elderly widower in the afternoon. He would already have his evening meal place setting on the table, ready for the meal that was still several hours away.

My wife and I stayed in the guest room in an assisted living facility for several days while visiting my wife's mother, who was a resident. Immersing ourselves in the facility's daily activities, we observed the set routines for meals, baths, the dispensing of medications, exercise times, movie time, etc. Lots of routine. The residents, however, also formed their own unique routines in addition to the institutional routines. Most were not happy when those routines were interrupted or changed.

We seniors also need a lot less in our day to consider the day packed. Any additions to our schedule disrupt the day's routine. One doctor's appointment or a grocery store run is more than enough, prompting labeling the day an extraordinarily busy one. Don't suggest adding something else to such an already packed day.

No one likes interruptions, but we seniors find them especially upsetting. If there's to be an interruption, we'd like the interruption be put on the schedule, far in advance, please. Want us to be spontaneous? Only if we can schedule it, again, far in advance if possible.

As we grow older, having a diminishing number of responsibilities is common. This allows us the luxury of becoming more comfortable with a daily routine. Unfortunately, many with whom we relate on a regular basis are younger and have busy lives. They can't always accommodate our schedules or plans, and so we find we must yield to their time frame.

When I was a pastor, I left the house one morning, telling my wife I would be working on my sermon about the interruptible life. She said, "Maybe you'll get interrupted writing your sermon and have another illustration for the message." I replied, "I hope not." Then I thought, "Wow! I'll be speaking on living an interruptible life, and I don't want to be interrupted while writing the sermon!"

My preparation for that sermon revealed Jesus lived a very interruptible life. Yet his life was a perfect fulfillment of the heavenly Father's plans for him. The four gospels record some thirty-five miracles which Jesus performed. Almost every one, if not all, resulted from Jesus being interrupted.

On one occasion when Jesus was teaching, Scripture recounts, "While he was saying this, a ruler came and knelt before him and said, 'My daughter has just died. But come and put your hand on her, and she will live.' Jesus got up and went with him, and so did his disciples" (Matthew 9:18–19). Whatever they had planned, the plans just got changed.

We read further while they followed the grieving father to his home, "Just then a woman who had been subject to bleeding for twelve years came up behind him and touched the edge of his cloak. She said to herself, 'If I only touch his cloak, I will be healed.'" Another interruption. "Jesus turned and saw her" (vs. 20–22). His first interruption was interrupted by a second interruption. So, Jesus talks with the woman, then heals her. Finally arriving at the grieving father's house, Jesus raises his daughter back to life again, but not without the delay caused by the desperate woman.

If Jesus's miracles were usually not planned but resulted from interruptions, then what do we think our chance is of succeeding at following Jesus without being flexible? Faith in him requires flexibility in following him, even at an older age.

Have you ever been in a store, asked a clerk for help, feeling as if you were interrupting the clerk's work? I have. Do they not realize the customer is the reason they have a job in the first place?

Successful retail businesses operate on the expectation that customers will interrupt the shopkeeper. Stocking shelves, tidying up the store, working on the financial books, all such work stops when a customer walks in the door. I like what was written on yardsticks years ago that were given away by a lumber yard in the Midwest: "You are not an interruption to our business; you are our business."

Our resistance to interruptions can be a control issue—a refusal of accepting God's agenda for us. Do we want to do the Lord's business each day? One way God does his business with us is by interrupting what we're doing. What we see as an interruption of our plans is an appointment for carrying out God's plans. To be used by God, we must be interruptible. Woody Allen has been quoted as saying "If you want to make God laugh, tell him your plans."

While God has us here on earth, he has a plan, his purpose for us. This plan and purpose will not always fit neatly into the predetermined, comfortable schedule we have for our day. As a follower of Jesus, we should accept the implied disclaimer in his teachings *Your schedule is subject to change without notice.* Living out a faith in God requires we remain flexible. C. S. Lewis believed we should resist seeing unpleasant events as interruptions in our life. The truth, Lewis explained, is that our so-called interruptions make up our real life that he gives us day by day.

Being interruptible is a key to growing older gracefully. A growing faith and deepening trust in God can keep us flexible.

BEING A BEAUTIFUL BURDEN—
DAY 5

When my elderly mother lived alone in an apartment, she needed family help with getting her groceries, doing her finances (because she had failing vision), taking her to doctors' appointments, and doing the major house-cleaning. Because of their proximity, this needed help often came from my brother, sister, and my niece, one of my mother's granddaughters, Tracy. In a phone conversation, Mom shared with me what she had told Tracy. "You're doing God's work when you help me." Golden words from a woman in her golden years.

Frequently people exclaim, "I don't want to be a burden to anyone." The reality is God's call on our lives might include being a burden to others. Our need gives them the opportunity to carry out their calling from God by helping us carry our burden.

The apostle Paul stated, "The Lord Jesus himself said, 'It is more blessed to give than to receive'" (Acts 20:35). This great truth not only means we should serve others, so we are a blessing in their life, but that sometimes we must allow others the opportunity of giving themselves to us, so they can be blessed by being a blessing in our life.

As we grow older, we'll likely face an increasing need for dependence on others. If we succeed at surviving to a ripe old age, the chances are even greater we'll need more help.

Babies need help from others, but older people frequently need help from others as well—the youngest and the oldest, the bookends of life. People in between these two bookends of life are often called upon to offer care to the young and old. Theirs is a story of bearing a burden. We who are in our senior years—the last book on the shelf—might involve, as part of our story, being a burden to others, but it can be a beautiful burden.

Marilyn McEntyre, in her book, *A Faithful Farewell: Living Your Last Chapter with Love*, writes, "The Amish teach that the sick, the elderly, and the dying are gifts to the community because of the love and care they bring forth. That's a beautiful and generous way to think about what my 'contribution' may be now to a community in which I used to be much more 'useful.' Allowing others to be generous and tender, giving them occasion for the sacrifices of time and energy that deepen their investment in my life, may seem like a necessary evil, but perhaps it's a necessary good. I am still a participant."[2]

Joni Eareckson Tada, writer, speaker, and artist, has been a quadriplegic for over forty years. She depends on caretakers, including her husband, Ken, to survive ... and thrive. She has said that God designed her disability as a means for moving her from being independent to being interdependent.

We would prefer to see ourselves as helping someone rather than being helped. But the reality is, for every burden lifter, there's a person who has a burden and needs help lifting it. God does not tell us we should be indepen-

dent. Instead, the Bible calls for us to be, as Joni Eareckson Tada stated, "interdependent." The apostle Paul wrote, "Carry each other's burdens, and in this way you will fulfill the law of Christ" (Galatians 6:2).

Through the aging process, living independently as long as we can is our wish. However, there might come a time when this is no longer possible. Ironically, living independently to avoid being a burden on others when it's not realistic to do so might actually increase the burden we put on those who love us, who are concerned about us.

When we need help carrying our burden of aging, we should realize the humble acceptance of help is a powerful way the Lord is refining us, for it takes more grace to accept help than to give help. Being less of a burden on others is achieved by being grateful, cheerful, and encouraging instead of grumbling, apologizing, and complaining because we're in such a position. Yes, we can be a beautiful burden.

When I think of being a beautiful burden, I'm reminded of Rudy Holloman, a senior member in the church I served. He was a widower, lived alone, and was legally blind. His family was supportive, providing as much help as they could, but there were times when they weren't available to take Rudy to church or a doctor's appointment. This is where his church family came in.

To Rudy's credit, he wasn't afraid to ask for a ride from those in his church. Rudy remained quite mobile because people rarely turned down his request for a ride. He got to where he had to go, even where he wanted to go. They loved taking Rudy places, because Rudy was a fun person to be around. He was joyful and humorous. He also gave a homemade loaf of banana bread as a thank you gift to those who took him places.

A couple who often took Rudy to church and other places recalled how, when they were pushing him down a ramp in his wheelchair, he would raise his hands in the air shouting, "Whoopee!" Rudy was not a burden.

Unlike Rudy, we add to the burden on the person helping us by being so apologetic or depressed about needing help that we're no fun to be around. We can even go so far as being short tempered around our helper. That's when we become a real burden, the very thing we don't want to be.

Sure, asking for help is humbling. Bingo! Guess what attribute God wants us to develop? Humility. God's divine plan is we let ourselves be helped as well as being a helper. The apostle Paul, grateful for the financial help from the Christians at Philippi, wrote, "Yet it was kind of you to share my trouble" (Philippians 4:14).

We should see being dependent upon others as a type of sacrament. A sacrament is something tangible, physical, in which we participate that reminds us of something spiritual. Being dependent on others can, in a tangible way, remind us we're dependent on God, that his help is often being channeled through the people whose help we need. Allowing ourselves to be helped can be a sacramental experience for us.

Yes, serving others joyfully is important. However, just as important is joyfully accepting others serving us, a truth we should adopt as we navigate the senior years. I learned this from my mother, who saw her granddaughter "doing God's work" by helping her, and from my parishioner Rudy Holloman, who asked for help, giving away banana bread as a thank you.

RESPONSIBLE REMINISCING—DAY 6

We older folks love reminiscing; it's easy because we have so much material with which we can work. We've accumulated a lifetime of memories. It's hard to ignore these many memories, so we reminisce.

Reminiscing can be good. In fact, it's essential we remember and reflect upon the past, because the past made us who we are today. Imagine living with total amnesia, not remembering anything from years ago to a few moments ago. We'd be a conscious being, living in the moment, but with no sense of identity. Our past is a major part of who we are. Life would shrink to something very small if we knew only what was happening today.

Memories can contribute to living today well. Parker Palmer writes, "Calamities I once lamented now appear as strong threads of a larger weave, without which the fabric of my life would be less resilient. Moments of fulfillment I failed to relish in my impatience to get on to the next thing now appear as times to be recalled and savored."[3] Yes, the benefit of age is we can put both the bad and the good of the past in a better perspective. God can show us how the hurt in the past should impact us for the good in the present. He can also help us appreciate the blessings in the past, so they can bless us all over again.

However, the temptation is to live in the past, yearning for the good ol' days. But we can't do this. The past is past. Responsible reminiscing, then, is not *living* in the past but *building* on the past. "We can draw lessons from the past, but we cannot live in it" is a bit of wisdom often attributed to the late President Lyndon Johnson.

This responsible reminiscing should prompt thanksgiving, a crucial practice for any serious follower of God. Thanksgiving is rejoicing in our reminiscing. This is what the psalmist did. "I remember the days of long ago; I meditate on all your works and consider what your hands have done" (Psalm 143:5).

The beauty of growing older is we have an ever-increasing inventory of past experiences where the Lord came through for us. Reflecting on God's grace in bygone days, and his mercy through months long past, can bolster our confidence that he will see us through what we now face and will face. This is a significant reason why we can have joy in our later years.

The apostle Paul states, "Rejoice always, pray continually, give thanks in all circumstances; for this is God's will for you in Christ Jesus" (1 Thessalonians 5:16–18). Yes, we can rejoice always because God is at work in our lives as we remember him working in our past. We're to pray continually, being in constant communication and communion with him, confident his ever present presence in the past is also our current reality. We can give thanks in all circumstances, good or bad, because he will help us survive the present as he has the past.

Not everything in our past is a positive memory. Rose Kennedy, mother of the late President Kennedy, reportedly said, "Now I am in my eighties, and I have known the joys and sorrows of a full life. Age, however, has its privileges. One is to reminisce, and another is to reminisce selectively." We can choose what we dwell on in our past.

Still, there are experiences in our past that are painful and are not easily forgotten. Perhaps the painful memories involve the wrong behavior of others. Sometimes, there's the recollection of our own failures, mistakes, and sins. When reminiscing results in regretting, we should address how we look at this painful part in our past.

One reality we must face is we must give up hope of changing the past. Oscar Wilde is believed to have said, "No man is rich enough to buy back his own past." The famous American humorist and social commentator, Will Rogers, is credited as saying, "Don't let yesterday take up too much of today."

Though we can't change past pain, the good news is we can change how we look upon that painful past. One good perspective to adopt when pondering past pain is embracing the truth that God never wastes pain.

I remember drinking coffee at a large heavy wooden table in a coffee shop in Toledo, Ohio. On one end, etched into the wood, were the words, "Repurposed materials." God can repurpose our painful past for present and future good.

Jesus encountered a man who was demon possessed and cast out the demons. I call this man Cemetery Man because his demonic condition had him living among the dead, in a cemetery, naked. People had tried apprehending him, but he had such strength he broke the chains. Can you imagine the reputation he had in the community? The locals, when they saw Cemetery Man clothed and in his right mind because of Jesus's actions, were so fearful they asked Jesus to leave their area. Cemetery Man asked Jesus if he could go with him. Can you blame him? How could he live among the people in his home area, given his past life? Jesus's response to Cemetery Man? "Return home and tell how much God has done for you" (Luke 8:39). In our senior years, God wants us giving bold testimony of how he helps us move beyond our painful past so we might "tell how much God has done." We can do so when we're convinced of what Paul declared. "And we know that in all things God works for the good of those who love him, who have been called according to his purpose" (Romans 8:28).

Neither does our own sinful past need haunt us, for that is where the grace and mercy of God can come into play. When Christ is our Savior, we're set free from our sinful past. "If we confess our sins, he is faithful and just and will forgive us our sins and purify us from all unrighteousness" (1 John 1:9). We might have a long track record of many sins going into our older age, but they all are reasons for celebrating the Lord's forgiveness through his grace and mercy bestowed upon us.

Yes, our older age gives us much over which we can reminisce. We have the God-given choice to reminisce responsibly.

BLESS THE CHILDREN—DAY 7

When people are asked who was a significant influence on them growing up, it's remarkable how often they mention a grandparent, an elderly neighbor, or some other person who was a half century or more older. I've seen this so often that I call this "the skipped generation syndrome," meaning that oftentimes a grandparent or other elderly person can influence a child or young person in a way that the parents can't.

What an opportunity for us to continue impacting our world for good! No wonder the book of Proverbs says, "Children's children are a crown to the aged" (Proverbs 17:6).

Perhaps this unusual connection between the young and the old is because both generations are often marginalized. Parents with children and teenagers are the busy, distracted generation. If life were a river, parenting generations would be in the fast flow in the middle, navigating rough rapids, while the children and their grandparents would be in the slow-moving waters and swirling eddies along the shoreline. Neither the young nor the old are highly productive in society. They have more time on their hands. Yes, the young and old have much in common.

We who are grandparents and great-grandparents should embrace the wonderful truth that our influence on this younger generation is a significant part of our calling from God for this stage in our life. Even for those who are seniors but have no grandchildren, there is the opportunity for positive influence through nieces and nephews, a neighbor child, or some other young person within the sphere of influence. Our prayer should reflect the psalmist's prayer, "Even when I am old and gray, do not forsake me, my God, till I declare your power to the next generation, your mighty acts to all who are to come" (Psalm 71:18).

In the unfolding of God's kingdom, there's a strategic place for children. They are not to be marginalized. We seniors can keep them from being overlooked, following the examples of Simeon and Anna in the Bible. In the birth account of Jesus in Luke's gospel, the presentation of Jesus in the temple follows the familiar nativity story. Two main players come on the scene to bless Jesus and instruct Mary and Joseph concerning Jesus's unique personhood. God had told Simeon, presumably an older man, that he wouldn't die until he met the Messiah child. God had him present in the temple when the young family was there. Simeon took Jesus in his arms and praised God, giving a prophetic word to Mary and Joseph. Then, Luke wrote, there appeared an old woman, a prophetess named Anna. She gave thanks, declaring who this special child was. God the Father had two elderly people come forward to bless and speak concerning his Son Jesus.

Years later, as an adult, Jesus reprimanded his disciples for keeping the children from him, as if he were too important and busy to be bothered by children. He was not. Jesus said, "Let the little children come to me, and do not hinder them, for the kingdom of God belongs to such as these"

(Mark 10:14). Then we read, "He took the children in his arms, placed his hands on them and blessed them" (v. 16).

We who make up the oldest generation have a strategic calling to bless the children God puts within our sphere of influence. The psalmist proclaimed a hopeful blessing when he declared, "May you live to see your children's children" (Psalm 128:6). We're in a God-given position to be a blessing if we've been blessed by growing old enough to see our children's children or, if not having grandchildren, children of an equivalent age.

I asked my friends on Facebook to share the influence a grandparent or other older person had on them in their childhood years. A common theme was the grandparents had the time to give them focused attention. Liz wrote, "They gave me their full attention ... I felt valued, listened to, and profoundly loved." Hillary reflected, "I never once questioned their love for me. They always listened with genuine, undistracted interest." Kathie commented concerning her grandmother, "She said positive things to me. I knew she loved me by the way she treated me."

Two responses came from cousins who shared the same grandmother, Verna Kay, a long-time member of the church I served. Verna and her husband had reared five sons. She now had a large contingent of grandchildren. While visiting her, I listened as she shared her concerns for her large family. Now widowed, her whole life was wrapped around the Lord, her children, their spouses, and her grandchildren. She had a deep faith and was the spiritual matriarch in the family. Granddaughter Michelle wrote, "Before she passed away, we had a conversation I will cherish forever. First, she told me that life goes so incredibly fast and to always be present and trust in the Lord. She then told me how proud she was of me as a beautiful and strong woman (and mother)." Granddaughter Danielle shared, "She was our prayer warrior ... She would tell us how much she loved Jesus, she would pray, talk to Jesus, and share the gospel to all whom God sent her way ... and allowed her faith in the Lord to be a bright and shining light for all to see!"

As the older generation, we have wonderful opportunities for expressing God's glory and doing his good to the younger generation. The psalmist declared, "But from everlasting to everlasting the Lord's love is with those who fear him, and his righteousness with their children's children" (Psalm 103:17). We might no longer be as productive in as many ways as we were in our younger years, but we're in a position as never before to leave a legacy of the Lord and of love.

THE GIFT OF SLOWED TIME—DAY 8

Pastor and writer Calvin Miller wrote in his memoir, "I'll stop looking ahead and look around more."[4] He wrote these wise words later in life, when he was old enough to write a memoir. Growing older often means life slows, sometimes not, but most times, yes.

I sometimes ride my bicycle or take a walk on a road that I frequently drive with the car. I see, hear, and smell so much more when I travel the same mile on a bicycle or on a walk rather than in a car. Growing older is like traveling each day more at the speed of a bicycle or a walk rather than that of a car. The slowed pace offers the luxury of stopping and smelling the roses.

Yes, growing older can give the gift of slowed time. We older folks often have the time for embracing the moment and hugging the hour.

True, everyone has the same number of hours, minutes, and seconds in a day. However, we who are in the senior years aren't as likely to cram as much into a given time as those who are in the child-rearing and working years. We can't slow time, the clock ticks at the same tempo for everyone, but we can move along the timeline at a slower pace.

A comparison is moving from microwave living to slow cooker living.

I'm wondering what would happen if an ant and a snail, meeting beneath a mushroom, could bridge the communication gap between species, having a conversation about time. Would the ant tell the snail he's living nearly a stationary life? Would the snail tell the ant he's but a blur going by? Time might be the same for both the ant and the snail, but it appears they experience time differently. Humans are the highest order of God's created species, way above the ant and the snail. We have the God-given ability to choose how we handle the time we've been given on this earth.

Hurried living seems the norm but doesn't always pay off. There's the story of a man who hiked to the riverbank to catch a ferry. When he came around the last bend, he caught sight of the ferry that was about six feet from the dock. "I'm too late," he thought to himself, then realized he could jump the distance from the dock to the ferry, so he ran as fast as he could. At the dock's edge, he pushed himself into the air with all his might. He landed hard on the ferry's deck, much relieved. The ferry pilot said, "Great jump! You made it. But you could have just waited. I'm coming in, not going out." Hurried living is not always helpful for living well. In fact, we can, in our later years, find delight in taking a slower pace.

Years ago, my wife and I spent several days tent camping in Turkey Run State Park in Indiana. The area has about two dozen covered bridges, built in the late 1800s or early 1900s. Each bridge has its name painted on both ends, along with the reminder, "Cross the Bridge at a Walk." The warning goes back to the horse and buggy days. People believed that letting horses run across the bridge would cause enough vibration to damage the bridge.

People were often in a hurry way back then, much as they are today. Now more than ever, we should take the warning to heart. Instead of "Cross the Bridge at a Walk" we might say "Take Life at a Walk." We who are in our senior years are in the best place for putting this into practice, modeling it for those who are younger.

For three years, Jesus journeyed around a significant part of what we now call the Holy Land. We read in the Gospels that he walked or took a boat from place to place, frequently with his disciples alongside him. We don't have record that he ever jogged. They didn't have speed boats back then. The disciples, if they were to follow him as he instructed them, had to set their pace to match their Master's.

The slower pace during the senior years allows for experiencing the Lord's presence more deeply. He is with us, and we are with him every moment. At a slower pace, our moments with Him are sweeter. The psalmist affirmed, "Blessed are those who have learned to acclaim you, who walk in the light of your presence, Lord. They rejoice in your name all day long; they celebrate your righteousness" (Psalm 89:15–16).

Once, I found a tortoise on the campground where we stayed. Being a serious amateur photographer, I'm always looking for interesting and creative images to photograph. In this case, I placed my wristwatch on the tortoise's back, then took its picture.

"Tortoise Time" is the title I gave the image. We seniors can rejoice in having given up much of the rat race to living more at the tortoise's speed.

Unless we have an early doctor's appointment or must watch the grandkids, we usually don't have to jump start the day with the alarm clock. We can slowly drift into consciousness, though a demanding full bladder might speed up that awakening process. What a blessing to retire the alarm clock when we retire.

The blessing of a leisurely pace means we can allow more time for reading. Regular trips to the library can become part of the weekly routine. A slower pace also gives an opportunity for exploring extended time in prayer. My daily prayer walk formerly was about twenty minutes in length. Now, it is about an hour. A relaxed pace can afford us the option for connecting with people more, either in person, by phone, through email, messaging, or even texting.

The blessing of slowed time provides us with opportunities for blessing those around us who are younger and in the rush hours of their lives. When they're with us, they *must* slow their pace to match ours if there's to be any meaningful relating, especially if we refuse to increase our pace. We can gently help them slow their racing thoughts, transforming them into reflective thoughts, even if for a short time, replacing some rushing with some resting. When they share a meal with us, they're not "grabbing lunch" but savoring a meal.

Slowed time as a senior also means we can give our undivided attention to others. We don't have one eye on the clock, so we can focus both eyes on the one with whom we're in conversation. We have time for listening, for building in long pauses between what they say and our response. This is a precious gift for the children in our sphere of influence. Their parents are often busy, sometimes distracted. We can fill the gap.

Arrival in our senior years brings with it the sobering reality we don't have unlimited time here on earth. This perspective can prompt a deeper appreciation for the time we have left, intentionally holding on to each moment, embracing it, making the most of it. We don't have to rush on to what's next but can appreciate what's now. This is unwrapping the gift of slowed time.

KEEP LEARNING—DAY 9

"You can't teach an old dog new tricks" is a saying that's been around a long time but is a false statement. A study was done in Austria with ninety-five border collies ranging in age from five months to thirteen years. The study showed that, yes, the younger dogs learned faster, but the older dogs could still learn. A better saying to adopt is "You're never too old to learn."

Learning takes time, and a slower pace helps. We seniors often have more time and that slower pace we can give toward learning.

Think about the different way people use park trails. Often at the trail head, park rangers provide a brochure for a self-guided hike that identifies various points of interest and explains something about them. Those who take the brochure will occasionally stop and read the brochure, look, touch, even smell specific points of interest. These people take their time in traveling the trail. Others jog the trail, huffing and puffing past the person standing there with the brochure. Two business men, dress shirt sleeves rolled up, talk business as they take a break from the office, walking the trail. Two mothers pushing strollers are in deep conversation about their children as they navigate the strollers over the bumpy path. Lovers walk the trail, hand in hand, giggling, teasing each other, and stopping to steal a kiss.

All come out at the end of the trail, but the joggers, businessmen, mothers, and lovers never experienced much of what the trail had to offer. They didn't learn about the unique bird's nest high in a tree or that the moss on the ground is found nowhere else in the world. Those with the brochure experienced the amazing and wonderful scenery scattered along the path, learning a thing or two along the way.

We in the geriatric years often have more opportunity for emulating those with the educational brochure while taking the hike. The last part of life's journey called the senior years can be a time for expanded learning. These opportunities for learning can come from many directions. Seniors can often take advantage of free community college classes. Our schedules allow for more frequent trips to the library or bookstores. Documentaries are available on cable TV or the internet. We have the flexibility for taking one or more classes at our church. We can allow more time for personal Bible study and reflection.

We can also be intentional about finding opportunities through nature to be attentive to God speaking to us. Jesus often used nature as a teaching tool. Are we open to God doing the same with us? Watching birds feast at a bird feeder can remind us the Lord is a good provider for us, as Jesus stated in Matthew 6:26, "Look at the birds of the air; they do not sow or reap or store away in barns, and yet your heavenly Father feeds them. Are you not much more valuable than they?" A sunset with clouds edged in golden light can remind us of heaven. Watching a slow-moving slug can prompt reflection on how God might want to use our slower pace.

Our grandchildren, great-grandchildren, and other little ones can teach us so much. Our slower pace allows for such conversations. Out of the mouth of babes come fresh ways to look at things.

We can learn from teenagers. The common thought is that the elderly can bestow wisdom on the young, and that's true, but we can reverse the process, asking questions of the young people. This gives them the gift of our listening ear, a gift that will be returned with us learning something in the process.

We who are committed followers of Jesus are called his disciples. A disciple is a student, one who is willing to learn. Jesus calls us to the exciting prospect of learning and growing as we go through life, including the senior years. We never graduate from learning until God gives us our diploma as we enter heaven.

A good prayer for us to pray is Psalm 25:4–5: "Show me your ways, O Lord, teach me your paths. Guide me in your truth and teach me for you are God my Savior, and my hope is in you all day long."

Going through each day being attentive to God's communication is a great way to live. At every turn there are a multitude of ways God can be speaking, teaching, molding, and making us into someone more like him.

The senior years bring their own unique challenges, including health challenges. These medical issues provide opportunities for learning through the school of difficulties. God can teach us even in these problematic situations, the kind we'd rather not face.

John Newton, writer of the most famous Christian song, "Amazing Grace," wrote in a letter, "I suppose you have heard I have been ill—through mercy, I am now well. But indeed I must farther tell you, that when I was sick—I was well! And since the Lord has removed my illness—I have been much worse. My illness was far from violent, and was greatly sweetened by a calm submissive frame the Lord gave me under it. My heart seemed more alive to him then than it has done since my cough, fever, and deafness have been removed."[5] John Newton experienced amazing grace, so he could learn that when he was sick, he was well.

We can learn things in difficult times that we won't learn in easy times. The golden years aren't always golden, as has often been said, but they provide a golden opportunity for learning lessons we've not learned before.

Even amid hurt, pain, and suffering, we can hear from God. In fact, as C. S. Lewis stated, pain is often God's megaphone. Life's journey is a journey through a fallen world, but God can show us so much on that journey, including during the last part of that journey, if we but have eyes with which to see, ears with which to hear, an open mind, and receptive heart.

KEEP REACHING OUT—DAY 10

Oftentimes the elderly will lament, "I've outlived all my friends." As a pastor for almost forty years, I had several funerals, most were graveside services, where only a couple of people were in attendance. The deceased had outlived all relatives and friends. Because there were so few people, I acted as one of the pallbearers, helping carry the casket from the hearse to the grave. The obvious solution to this dilemma is the continual acquisition of younger friends as we grow older. This requires intentional effort on our part.

The tendency in modern culture is to isolate seniors in retirement villages, senior apartments, assisted living facilities, and nursing homes. Such lifestyles might be necessary, perhaps even fulfilling, but they're not conducive for establishing new friendships with the younger generation. However, this is not impossible. We might feel age has marooned us on the island of isolation, but we can still build bridges to the mainland with the younger generations.

Those living in senior facilities can make an effort at becoming acquainted with the younger generations who make up the staff of the facility. These younger staff have lives beyond their workplace. They'll be delighted to be treated as more than just a staff person responsible for meeting the senior citizens' needs. They have mates, families, problems, interests, and hobbies. When related to as a real person, they'll most likely respond with genuine care, concern, and love, which allows for the development of true friendships.

Living the "golden years" often means more frequent trips to doctors and medical facilities, where we'll frequently interact with the same medical staff. Why not make the effort of building relationships with these staff members? As a pastor, I had numerous medical staff in my church who frequently described with terms of endearment patients they had come to know and love. We can be such a patient.

Medical and elder care personnel become a new and growing circle of acquaintances for us seniors. But they can be more than a parade of unwelcome people, which our age demands we let tend to our infirmities. They're part of our sphere of influence, people brought into our lives for whom we can add value by being gracious, joyful, and loving.

I recall several funeral home visitations where medical or assisted living staff came, paying their respects. With much emotion, they shared about their special relationship with the person we were remembering and honoring. They were the helpers of the deceased, but felt they had received so much more in return.

We seniors who still live independently, or with a family member, have neighbors who are younger. We can be a good neighbor, adding value to their lives. People love having older neighbors when those older neighbors aren't old grumps.

When John and Patty moved into their neighborhood many years ago, they were the youngest people on the street. Patty writes, "I was incredibly blessed to be bookended on our street by two of the loveliest elderly women, whom I considered to be very dear friends.

"Polly lived every day fully, graciously, and lovingly right up to her last day at age ninety-four. She used to have frequent parties, and we always knew the age ranges would be from twenty-five to ninety-five, and people from all walks of life.

"Louise always had the same huge smile, hearty laugh, and sparkle in her eyes. She was a Carnegie Mellon graduate, taught home economics, and was still trying out new recipes when she was a hundred—she lived to be a hundred and five. She sent a casserole home with me for John to try, and he said, 'What has this world come to that a hundred-year-old is sending us dinner!'

"They were a wealth of wisdom and kindness to me. Both women had friends of all ages throughout their lives, and to me, they were ageless."

We must silence the self-talk—"No one likes to be around an old person"—which is not true, for Patty, Polly, and Louise were ageless. If we're a kind, caring, and joyful person, people will enjoy being around us, no matter our age. We'll be ageless. We just need to be open to relationships with those younger than ourselves, intentional about reaching out to the younger generations.

My sister-in-law Sheila says, "One of the things I'm involved with is being a mentor for young mothers at MOPS (Mothers of Preschoolers). It's interesting to see how times have changed in some ways since I was home with my kids but also how things are still the same."

A retired friend of mine, Mitch, spends time discipling his twenty-one-year-old grandson and helping home school another grandson, who is seven years old. Mitch also regularly sits down for a meal with several men between fifty and sixty years in age. Mitch is by no means limiting his relationships to those his own age.

Volunteering at church, a food pantry, or some other worthy organization can expand our connections with people, people who are younger than we are. If health or other circumstances prohibit such active involvement, we can still reach out to others with a phone call, text, email, or by sending cards or letters. Occasionally, my wife will send our grandchildren a card through the mail, though they live near us. They're delighted to get real mail addressed to them. The younger generations get so few cards and letters it's a novelty that often makes it meaningful.

Praying for people is another way we can engage in others' lives We can pray from the comfort of our own home, sitting in our favorite chair. Prayer does change things—that's one reason the Bible tells us to make our requests known to God. We multiply the blessing of praying for someone by letting them know we did so. This encourages them, deepening our relationship with them.

The apostle Paul, as an old man, had a close relationship with a young man named Timothy. Paul loved Timothy as a son, and Timothy loved Paul. Paul, when separated from Timothy, wrote him, "I constantly remember you in my prayers. Recalling your tears, I long to see you, so that I may be filled with joy" (2 Timothy 1:3–4).

Paul believed, though old, he had much he could pour into the life of someone much younger. Paul saw this as part of his calling. We also can add value to the younger generations.

If the Lord has us here on his earth and hasn't called us home to heaven, he has plans for us. That calling includes reaching out to those he's placed around us, which often means those younger than us.

LIMITATIONS DON'T HAVE TO LIMIT—DAY 11

Every so often, I have the opportunity of walking along a sandy ocean shore, where waves and shore do battle about where the boundary should be. The roaring waves rush in, claiming new sandy territory, then retreat, losing ground to the terra firma, then rush back in again, reclaiming territory only to retreat again. The battle rages on through eons of time. Even a vast ocean has boundaries. So does land, the shoreline being the boundary for both. This is by God's design. Scripture says in Proverbs 8:29 that God "gave the sea its boundary."

God has also set his boundaries for our lives. Often, we don't like this. Children, when asked what they want to be or do when they grow up, will often rattle off a diverse list of adventures and careers, as if they can do it all. No one can. When we grow up, we realize this, sort of, but sort of not. Graduation speakers often do not help us here, encouraging those graduating that they can do whatever they can dream. Not so!

A sight-impaired person can't be a fighter pilot. A person who has trouble with math will likely never be a great mathematician. A heavyweight boxer can't switch careers, becoming a race horse jockey.

Health issues can limit us. Financial resources sometimes are a limiting factor. Geography also limits us (you can't enjoy snow skiing if living in Florida or swimming with the dolphins if living in Minnesota).

Growing older means facing a growing list of limitations. Our bodies won't let us do what we did when younger; they are also more finicky about what we eat or drink. Thinking processes seem to slow, multitasking becomes more difficult, and memory fails us more often. We might have to give up driving or living independently.

Life serves up new limits as we get older, and we don't like those limits. We bristle at boundaries, fixating on what we can't do or can't be, envying those younger who still have many options.

One of the greatest Christians who ever lived was the apostle Paul. He not only was a great preacher, teacher, and church planter, but was also used by the Lord to heal people. We read, "God did extraordinary miracles through Paul, so that even handkerchiefs and aprons that had touched him were taken to the sick, and their illnesses were cured and the evil spirits left them" (Acts 19:11–12). Paul's ministry must have been amazing.

Yet, Paul faced limitations, suffering from an ailment. He called it a "thorn in my flesh." He undoubtedly felt inhibited doing the Lord's work. He wrote the Corinthian Christians, "Three times I pleaded with the Lord to take it away from me" (2 Corinthians 12:8). Remember, this is the guy who God used mightily to heal others. They were even healed if they touched a handkerchief he had touched. Paul only asked that the Lord do for him what the Lord had done for others through him. He set aside three specific times, probably with intense praying and very likely fasting, asking the Lord to heal him. Then he heard the Lord Jesus Christ tell him, "My grace is sufficient for you, for my power is made perfect in weakness" (v.9). The implied answer for Paul from the Lord was a clear "No." The Lord would not heal him of that which Paul undoubtedly thought limited his effectiveness for serving the Lord.

Paul then shares his response concerning the new reality that he would live with his "thorn in the flesh." He writes, "Therefore I will boast all the more gladly about my weaknesses, so that Christ's power may rest on me. That is why, for Christ's sake, I delight in weaknesses, in insults, in hardships, in persecutions, in difficulties. For when I am weak, then I am strong" (vs. 9–10).

Paul realized his greatest satisfaction would not come from the removal of his limitation but from the Lord's gracious help living with his limitation. Jesus had promised Paul his grace would be sufficient for Paul. Jesus's response is recorded in our Bibles so we can hear the same message from Jesus. Yes, we senior citizens are facing new limitations. Jesus's words are for us, as they were for Paul: "My grace is sufficient for you, for my power is made perfect in weakness."

While Diann and I were hiking a trail in a western national park, we met an older couple also hiking the trail. I can't recall if I was catching my breath, telling him and his wife to pass, or how we ended up standing there in a short conversation with them. Turns out he was eighty-one years old. He walked with a cane and had a leg brace, but this didn't slow him. He shared with us how he had both knees and a hip replaced. A while later, I saw him head toward the restrooms. One was marked "Handicapped," but he didn't use this one. He entered the regular restroom.

What a guy, I thought. He had all these physical issues, walked with a leg brace and a cane, but didn't see himself as being handicapped. I want to be like him when I grow up. (Just a note here: Handicap restrooms are necessary for many people, who would have a difficult time using a regular facility. I suspect this gentleman, during his recovery from his different health issues, also used handicap restrooms. My point is, by God's grace, he apparently no longer felt he needed the special facilities.)

This elderly hiker with the cane and leg brace reminded me that limitations don't have to limit us. We can't always control what happens to us, but we can always control how we respond to what happens to us. How limitations impact us has far more to do with our attitude than with the circumstances themselves.

We might think our limitations limit us, but God is not limited by our limitations. In fact, he can do things with us and our limitations he couldn't do with us without our limitations. We limit God's plan for us when we complain or grumble about our growing limitations as we grow older.

There's a better approach. Boundaries define what we can be and should do. As we grow older, we can, by God's grace, affirm that limitations don't have to limit us or bind us. They can be a guide to God's best for us. We can affirm with the psalmist, "Lord, you alone are my portion and my cup; you make my lot secure. The boundary lines have fallen for me in pleasant places; surely I have a delightful inheritance" (Psalm 16:5–6).

THE SENIOR MOMENT OF SETTING AN EXAMPLE—DAY 12

In a faraway land long ago, a man prepared to take his elderly father up a mountain with plans for leaving him there to die, something they did in those days in that land. The man's son asked if he could go with his father when he took the boy's grandpa up the mountain to die.

"Why do you want to go with me?" the boy's father asked.

The boy replied, "So I know where to take you when you get old like Grandpa."

This is a fictitious story, but it's a reminder the younger generations are watching us.

Sometimes, as older folks, we might feel marginalized—invisible to the younger generations with their busy and hectic lives. We, in the more sedentary stage of the senior years, can feel as if we're nothing but an indistinguishable blur to the younger, more hurried generations, like the view out a side window from a fast-moving vehicle. We should think again. They're watching us even though we believe we're being ignored. We might not have the focus of their attention, but they're watching us with their peripheral vision.

We who are parents were aware, when we were young parents, that our children were watching, often copying us. Now that our children are adults, and we're old, we should remember our children still watch us—how we handle this last stage of life. Are we setting a good example or a bad one? Will they copy our example in their old age? Should they?

We talk about having senior moments when we forget something or get a bit confused. But there's another kind of senior moment—that moment when our adult children, grandchildren, great-grandchildren, or others watch how we handle a situation, especially a situation unique for someone our age. The senior years provide many such telling circumstances: retiring, needing help around the house and yard, giving up driving, moving to assisted living, being diagnosed with a serious health issue, dealing with the loss of a mate, and the final challenge in facing death. We cannot know, for certain, how we'll handle any senior situation. But we can determine, by God's grace, we will face them in a way that brings glory to God and good to those who watch us.

Now that I'm a senior citizen, I often think back on how my grandparents, then my parents (all now deceased), handled being the age I now am and the age I'm growing into. My memory prompts a reflecting on how my children, grandchildren, and great-grandchildren will view how well I'm doing at being old.

We're living out our life on a stage, during all our lifetime, but no truer than when the process of aging has transformed us into the senior actors in this drama called life. We always have an audience—those in our sphere of influence. They have a free ticket of admission by the fact they know us. They're watching to see how we play the final act before the curtain falls. Part of our job description as an older player in the drama of life, like it or not, is setting an example of how to play the elder. That example can be good or bad. The choice is ours.

The apostle Paul wrote what I think is a bold, brazen, and bodacious statement to the Christians in Corinth, "Follow my example, as I follow the example of Christ" (1 Corinthians 11:1). I'm not sure I'd want to say that to anyone, but Paul did, and I'm working toward that goal. My goal is to tell those within my sphere of influence, "As you see me dealing with the issues that come with growing older, follow my example when it's your turn." Like Paul wrote, the key is having my example be based on Christ's example, whom I follow as a Christian. I want the light of his presence illuminating my life for the good of those he's placed around me.

One day while taking a walk, I saw a beetle crawling across my path. The sun was just up. The beetle was walking away from the sunrise, the sun casting a long shadow in front of him. He was a good-sized beetle as beetles go, but still a small object. I could have inadvertently stepped on him. We think of shadows being cast by big objects like clouds, trees, and buildings, but here a small bug cast a big shadow.

You can't have a shadow without light. Light is an important metaphor in the Bible. God is described as brilliant light. Jesus called himself the light of the world, inviting his listeners to walk in his light. We also are called to walk in his light and in the light of his Word.

Back to the little beetle casting a shadow bigger than himself. The angle of light in which he basked dictated the shadow size.

Shadows have no substance, no weight, no texture, and are one dimensional. They shift location with the moving sunlight that casts them. Yet they can be helpful when we give them another name, shade, a good place to stand when the day is hot and sunny.

Sometimes as seniors, we can feel we're no longer useful or have value. This is not true. No matter how small, insignificant, or unimportant we sometimes feel, when we continue drawing near to God, the light of his presence means we cast a larger shadow of influence than we ever thought possible. We're not big or important in and of ourselves, but the light of his presence makes us so. Yes, there can be many senior moments when Christ's light can be a real blessing for us and for those who watch us.

SHIFTING FROM A HUMAN DOING TO A HUMAN BEING—DAY 13

George Burns was a comedian who lived to be a hundred years old. During his last years, much of his humor was about being old. He often said, at his age, he got applause for simply showing up. What George Burns found to be true will likely be our experience as well. Our advancing years mean more people will expect less of us in terms of what we do. They're just happy we showed up.

Years ago, I attended a Christian conference. Along with the speakers, they had two older gentlemen present who were well known pastors, now retired. They were told by the conference organizers they had no specific ministry responsibility at the conference other than being sages. They both found being labeled sages rather humorous but took their assignment seriously by carrying out a ministry of wandering around, sitting around, listening, and chatting. They had a ministry focused on being rather than doing. As a much younger pastor, I benefited from their ministry of being there for me.

Being a senior at social gatherings doesn't always require us showing up with a dessert or anything else. Just being there is enough.

I call this the ministry of showing up. We can become experts at this ministry. We can make sure we're seated in the audience when the grandchild, nephew, niece, or neighbor child is on stage. The glancing look from the child, finding us in the audience, giving a quick smile or an understated back and forth wave of the hand is confirmation we still have a place in this world.

We can make ourselves available for the last-minute request to watch the child or children, so Mom, Dad, or both can rush off, taking care of an emergency or enjoying a surprise opportunity. We can sit, listening while the young reader struggles with sounding out word in a children's book. We can ask teenagers about the latest technology involving the smartphone that seems surgically attached to their hands. We can do so much by just being there.

For most people, life is focused on doing, accomplishing, and producing. This often requires squeezing much activity into little time, putting those short periods of time end to end, creating a burdensome chain of long hours. Observing so many around us rushing here, there, and back again, we nod our heads thinking *been there, done that.* Now our role is different, the accumulating years granting us the license as slower moving sages for those whose lives swirl around us at dizzying speed.

Sometimes, we might think we're being pushed to the sidelines by those living at a hectic pace, unnoticed, feeling they have little time for us. All this might be true, but there will also be those times when they will notice us, looking upon our slowed presence for counterbalance. We become an oasis offering the place with a slowed pace where they can, for the moment, pause finding some rest and restoration.

The situation does not require we have any words of wisdom, though we might. Our listening ear and attentive gaze could be what they need most. Even more important might be the open invitation they know we offer of sitting together and talking, or maybe just sitting together.

The example, both good and bad, of Job's friends is worth noting. The book of Job describes Job's great losses and suffering. When his three friends, Eliphaz, Bildad, and Zophar hear of Job's tragic state they come to visit. The text says, "Then they sat on the ground with him for seven days and seven nights. No one said a word to him, because they saw how great his suffering was" (Job 2:13). What a great example. They were three humans who were just *being* there with Job. Then, each in turn, started sharing their insights and advice with Job. They had been much more helpful when they just sat with Job, being with him. When they transitioned from being with Job to doing for Job (by opening their mouths to give advice), they stopped helping Job with his problems and began adding to his problems. Their presence was far more comfort than their words were helpful.

Best-selling author Parker Palmer, a person of senior rank, writes, "Don't give advice, unless someone insists. Instead, be fully present, listen, and ask the kind of questions that give the other a chance to express more of his or her own truth, whatever it may be."[6]

The tendency for those who are older and think we are wiser is to give those younger than us a piece of our mind or a slice from our experience from our own life. There could be a place for this, but not as big a place or as often as we might think.

This should encourage us when we feel we don't have any answers to offer or profound advice to give, or we might sense people aren't open to our input or advice. We can feel unimportant or even useless, especially if this a consistent pattern. But author Jocelyn Soriano states, "Remember this whenever you think that you have nothing worth giving. You always have something to give, a very valuable gift indeed. Consider giving people the very gift of your presence."[7]

Growing older means we have a growing opportunity to add value to people's lives by just showing up, by being there with them and for them. Growing older means we shift from a human doing to a human being. Our very presence can be silent words of help and encouragement loudly spoken.

A NEW CALLING—DAY 14

Retirement often means we've retired from a job or a career. We're no longer bound by the responsibility of showing up at work for so many hours for so much pay. What do we do now we're retired, no longer getting paid for showing up anywhere? Earning a living isn't a factor compelling us to get up in the morning. So, now we're retired, what will we do, and why will we do it? Unencumbered by a job, what motivates us?

An image symbolizing motivation is a carrot dangling on a string from a stick hung in front of a donkey pulling a cart. The man on the cart keeps the dangled carrot just beyond the donkey's reach. Each step the donkey takes moves the cart forward—also the dangling carrot. The donkey, not being the brightest animal in the barnyard, is motivated to keep pulling the cart forward to get the carrot, which remains just beyond reach.

What's the carrot dangled in front of us? Is there more than one carrot?

T. S. Elliot asked in 1941, "Can a lifetime represent a single motive?" He asked a good question. Can we live by one supreme, all-encompassing motive? Is there one carrot?

Os Guinness, who quoted the previous statement by Elliot, responded, "If the single motive is the master motivation of God's calling, the answer is yes."[8]

Being free from investing hours each week in a job means we can take a fresh look at what we want to do with these hours. The hectic pace of earning a living is in the past. The new calm from not rushing off to work gives us the opportunity for clarity we didn't have before in identifying what is important in life to us.

We might still have demands placed upon us by family, friends, church, perhaps a part-time job, clubs, and other organizations. But most of us possess time previously occupied by a job that now can be filled with something else. What is that something else going to be?

Many in retirement see this newfound freedom as an opportunity to do what they want to do. The question retirees often ask themselves is, "What do I want to do with my time?" We who are followers of Jesus Christ, who believe we are called by him, should realize this is not the right question. The right question is something to the effect of, "Lord, what do you want me to do with this newly freed up time you've given me?" For us Christians, our time is not our own, time is his, gifted to us, a gift for the unwrapping, intended for his glory and the good of the people he's placed within our sphere of influence. What we do with our retirement is not up to us, but up to him. What is he calling us to do in our retirement?

When we held down a job or had a career, it was right and good for us to frame what we did for a living as part of our calling from God. Any job, if it's not immoral, can be seen as a calling. Janitors, bankers, brick layers, salesclerks, farmers, nurses, stay-at-home parents, schoolteachers, custodians, etc., should see their work as a calling as much as does a pastor or missionary. God calls people to all kinds of work. All work is divine work carried out on sacred ground.

For the follower of Christ, the fundamental calling is the same in retirement as during the working years, living for his glory and the good of his people, carrying this out in specific ways in our current circumstances.

When we retire, we move beyond the calling to earn a living. We now have a new calling, yet the same calling, living for God, just in some new ways.

We can take encouragement from Moses. He lived for a hundred and twenty years, living in Egypt approximately the first forty years of his life. From age forty to age eighty, he was a shepherd tending his father-in-law Jethro's sheep in the land of Midian. Moses was eighty years old when he received his call from God to lead the Israelites out of Egypt. He would retire as a shepherd at age eighty, but God had a great work for Moses still to accomplish. Moses resisted. "But Moses said to God, 'Who am I, that I should go to Pharaoh and bring the Israelites out of Egypt?'" (Exodus 3:11). God had to convince him. Moses finally accepted his new calling. In our retirement years, we too might be tempted to ask, "Who am I?" Who am I that I should have anything worth contributing in this world at this stage of life? The fact is, we're never too old to have the call of God upon our lives.

This fresh calling from God can be exciting, but many times also scary as well as bewildering. Scary in that we likely are less adaptable and flexible the older we get. Being "set in our ways" can be a real issue. Bewildering in that we're not accustomed to having so much discretionary time requiring making choices as to how best to use this time.

Both fear and bewilderment can paralyze us from taking significant, intentional action. We can float from one hour to the next, from one day to the next, with no clear focus or agenda. A sense of purposelessness or even depression can creep up on us.

This transition from working to retirement can be as exciting, scary, and confusing as the transition was from being a teenager living with parents to entering adulthood, living on our own, and launching into higher education or a job. Most see this transition from teenager to adulthood as packed with possibilities. We should see our transition from working to retirement as packed with possibilities— an opportunity for asking afresh of the Lord, "What would you have me do?"

However, in these later years, the options seem a lot fewer than they did when we left home as a young person, beginning the adventure of adulthood. Launching into seniorhood can mean facing new financial issues, health issues, downsizing in various ways—changes that seem to shrink our world rather than expand it.

But no matter what our circumstances, until the Lord sees fit to call us home to his heaven, he has us here for a purpose. Even in our senior years, ours is still a called life.

There's a prayer by an unknown author we would do well to adopt as our own as we navigate our senior years.

> Lord, I am willing to receive what you give;
> To lack what you withhold;
> To relinquish what you take;
> To suffer what you inflict;
> To be what you require.

THE GIFT OF GROWING OLDER— DAY 15

The senior years are a gift not everyone receives. We who have reached a ripe older age can come up with a list of people we've known about our own age, some younger, who are no longer with us. Yet, here we are, still alive, having survived accidents, illnesses, and who knows what else.

We all have a little of the Mr. Magoo cartoon character in us. You remember, Mr. Magoo was vision impaired, his life being one adventure after another involving near misses with tragedy of which he was oblivious. When we arrive in heaven, we'll find out—maybe—if it's important for us to know, just how many times the Lord saved us from death.

Why we've survived until now, when many we know have not, is a mystery. Nothing happens or doesn't happen without God's action or consent, so we are still here because God has willed it so. How should we feel about this?

Because we know, as committed followers of Jesus, that we go to heaven when we die, we should have a different perspective on death than people who don't embrace Christ. Ultimately, we should get to the point in life where we can take it or leave it.

The apostle Paul expressed this ambivalence. "For to me, to live is Christ and to die is gain. If I am to go on living in the body, this will mean fruitful labor for me. Yet what shall I choose? I do not know! I am torn between the two: I desire to depart and be with Christ, which is better by far; but it is more necessary for you that I remain in the body" (Philippians 1:21–24). Paul was torn between the desire of going to heaven and meeting the Lord, or staying here on earth, being a help to the Lord's people. Paul concluded it was the Lord's will he stay around, helping God's people, though he was also okay with going to heaven.

As we grow older, moving closer to our time for transitioning from this life on earth to life with the Lord in heaven, we should be looking forward to that event with increasing anticipation. The fact is, like Paul, the Lord has us here on earth for the time being. Yes, desiring additional time here on earth is okay. In fact, we have a God-given instinct for survival. This drive for self-preservation is what keeps us from walking out into traffic.

However, a person can feel the opposite way as well, that there's not much to live for, that the painful struggles with aging outweigh the joys of living. I saw posted on the internet, "I finally figured out what I want to be when I get older ... Younger!" But we can't grow younger; growing older is our only option, other than the option of leaving this world, and, for some, this seems the better option.

A husband and wife arrived in heaven at the same time. The wife exclaimed, "This is so wonderful. I wish we could have come sooner." The husband replied, "We could have if you hadn't insisted on us eating all those oat bran muffins!"

The fact is we are here, regardless of how we feel about the matter, whether desiring more of this life or yearning for heaven. If we believe in God's sovereignty, then we are here because he wants us here. He has his purposes for us in this life, and until his purposes for us are fulfilled we are immune to death.

John Newton, pastor and author of the hymn "Amazing Grace," wrote a friend, "But I hope our work is not yet done; and, if not, I know the most dangerous disease cannot affect our life. Until the Lord's purposes by us and concerning us, are fulfilled—we are in perfect safety, though on a field of battle, or surrounded by the pestilence."[9]

Someday soon, we will enjoy his gift of eternal life in heaven, but for now, we should enjoy his gift of life on earth. When we see little value in our existence in the here and now, we're rejecting a gift from God, the gift of this life. We're being rude to God, like the receiver of a gift who communicates no appreciation to the gift giver for the gift.

Sure, the senior years have challenges, many new to this stage of life. As actress Betty Davis said, "Old age ain't no place for sissies." We can rattle off reasons why the "golden years" aren't so golden. Andy Rooney, American television broadcaster, is often credited with writing, "It's paradoxical that the idea of living a long life appeals to everyone, but the idea of getting old doesn't appeal to anyone."

Here is where we can use God's gift of choice, choosing how we'll handle our challenging senior years. Can we turn our grumbling into gratitude? We can if we choose to practice gratitude, finding ways to be thankful for the good we can still experience while the Lord has us on his earth.

"Forget not all his benefits" is what the psalmist declares in Psalm 103:2. We must break the habit of ungratefulness. Most of us have reminded children over the years to say "thank you" when given something, helping them establish the habit of being grateful. Now is the time to remind ourselves to do the same, replacing grumbling with gratitude.

King David affirmed in his most famous psalm these words, "Surely your goodness and love will follow me all the days of my life, and I will dwell in the house of the Lord forever" (Psalm 23:6). God gifts us with his presence, his goodness, his love in this life. While anticipating dwelling with him forever in his heaven, let's embrace his gift of life in the here and now.

GROWING OLDER WITH GRACE—
DAY 16

Growing older should include growing in our understanding of many things. There is no more important area for this to be true than in understanding we are the recipient of God's grace. This little book is titled *Growing Older Gracefully*. Let's focus on that last word in the title, "gracefully." Play with it a little. As we noted on the first day of our journey, "gracefully" is from the word "graceful." If you read the two parts of the word "graceful" in reverse order you have the concept of being full of grace.

One could assume this book's title, *Growing Older Gracefully*, means growing older in a "pleasing and attractive way," which is one definition for the word grace. This is the objective of this small volume, but the way this is achieved is by growing in our understanding of being the recipient of God's grace. We should be filled with God's grace, full of his grace, to be grace-full.

Grace not only means "pleasing and attractive," but also "undeserved favor." When we're referring to "grace" as an attribute of God, this can become personal for us. We're recipients of God's undeserved favor.

Why focus on God's grace as a subject in a book about growing older in pleasing and attractive ways? Because this growing older can best happen when we perceive how God has been gracious toward us, showing us undeserved favor in so many pleasing and attractive ways. Wayne Grudem writes, "The blessing of 'grace' upon Paul's readers is the most frequent apostolic blessing in his letters."[10] God's grace permeated Paul's letters. In fact, he uses the word "grace" at both the beginning and ending of all his letters. Grace should also permeate our senior years.

The opposite perception, that we've earned the right to have good things happen to us in our older age, will have us growing older in other than pleasing and attractive ways. A sense of entitlement, that we've earned the right to pamper ourselves, doing what we want, can turn us into that old grump mentioned at the beginning of this volume.

The fact is, all we have that is good has come from God. We might feel we have worked for what we have, but God gave us the ability, opportunities, strength, wisdom, and everything else we needed to achieve these accomplishments. He's given us all we're living on, whether much or little, in terms of Social Security, pension, inheritance, part-time job, etc. Our income is a gift. "Every good and perfect gift is from above, coming down from the Father of the heavenly lights" (James 1:17). He has been gracious toward us. Our lives are filled full with his grace.

We sometimes have a difficult time identifying God's good gifts because we're fixated on what we see as not good in our lives. As we get older, the aches and pains increase along with more serious medical issues. We find ourselves having to give up things we previously enjoyed. When the golden years have lost their luster, we should remember God has not lost *his* luster. We still have him, "the Father of the heavenly lights"; he has us. "Despite all appearances, the universe is a product of personal love," Philip Yancey writes.[11] Yancey also states that "at the heart of sin lies a lack of trust that God intends the best for us."[12]

When our senior years are less than ideal, we are in the perfect place for putting our faith and trust in God as we have never done before. This is the time for affirming as never before that God is a gracious God. Our minds, hearts, and souls are like a cup that can be turned upside down or right side up under the water faucet. Turned upside down, our cup will remain empty. Turned right side up, we can fill the cup. When we turn ourselves upward toward the Lord, turning our minds, hearts, and souls right side up, he can fill us with his gracious presence.

The writer of Hebrews reminds us, "Therefore, since we have a great high priest who has ascended into heaven, Jesus the Son of God, let us hold firmly to the faith we profess. For we do not have a high priest who is unable to empathize with our weaknesses, but we have one who has been tempted in every way, just as we are—yet he did not sin. Let us then approach God's throne of grace with confidence, so that we may receive mercy and find grace to help us in our time of need" (Hebrews 4:14–16). God's throne is called "the throne of grace." It's where we "find grace" from him.

Our relationship with God can bear more fruit as we grow older, if we continue growing in our understanding of his grace expressed toward us. The apostle Paul reminded the Ephesian Christians concerning a truth we should also grasp as we grow older. "For it is by grace you have been saved, through faith—and this is not from yourselves, it is the gift of God—not by works, so that no one can boast" (Ephesians 2:8–9).

We have no claim to God's blessings, no matter how long we've been following him. We have not earned our salvation nor do our efforts over the years to follow him and live his way give us the right to demand anything from God. Nothing from him is payment to us, but a gift. All of it.

Let's appreciate God's gracious working in our lives. Here's a reminder to do so from the writer of Hebrews, "See to it that no one falls short of the grace of God and that no bitter root grows up to cause trouble and defile many" (Hebrews 12:15).

We don't have to be a grumpy, complaining, demanding, angry person in what people often describe as the declining years. We can grow older gracefully, filled fuller of God's grace, which unleashes his all-sufficient power in our growing weakness.

THE SACRAMENT OF REST—DAY 17

Before I sat down at the computer to start this chapter, I lay on the couch, taking a nap. No kidding, I really did.

The retirement years often mean a less rigid daily schedule. The flexibility allows for sitting and resting a bit. Retirement also means a midday nap is a real possibility. Then, too, we can wake up on our own in the morning without the startling intrusion of the alarm clock. All these options are contingent on scheduling time for taking care of the grandchildren, nieces, and nephews, or the neighbors' kids.

Our declining stamina as we age gives us the license for a greater, more flexible use of rest. We need not feel guilty, though it's tempting to do so. Our culture holds in high esteem those who get by on just a few hours of sleep. Bragging rights are for those who get little sleep. Those who try getting a good night's sleep or taking a nap often keep the fact to themselves out of embarrassment or guilt.

Studies show that over half of us in the United States are sleep deprived. This is not good. Studies have also shown if we don't get enough sleep, we are at higher risk for obesity, heart disease, diabetes, dementia, and a shortened life expectancy. Sleep debt, as it is sometimes called, can also cause increased anxiety.

Of course, we can get too much sleep. Neither too little nor too much sleep is good. A Harvard-based Nurses' Health Study found that seven or eight hours of sleep is about right, that five hours or less or nine or more hours of sleep resulted in worse performance in memory and thinking skills. We, who are in our senior years, are in a good place for recapturing a proper balance between wakefulness and sleep. Our senior years also give an opportunity for modeling this better balance to younger generations.

So, a nap can be good, contributing to a healthy balance between awake time and sleep time. We in our senior years can find our nighttime sleep interrupted more frequently with trips to the bathroom and bouts with insomnia. A nap can help us recapture some lost sleep. Studies have shown that a nap can improve memory, creativity, and help maintain a better attitude (so we don't turn into that old grump).

A Pew Research poll found a third of those in the United States take a nap. This holds true for those in their seventies, but about half in their eighties take a nap. So, you're not alone if you decide to take a nap.

Even Jesus took a nap. "Then he [Jesus] got into the boat and his disciples followed him. Suddenly a furious storm came up on the lake, so that the waves swept over the boat. But Jesus was sleeping" (Matthew 8:23–24). He must have been napping soundly, sleeping during one of the worst storms his disciples, some being seasoned fishermen, had ever seen. The disciples woke Jesus. He then stilled the storm and reprimanded his disciples for their lack of faith. If the Son of God could take a nap, then so can we.

You might not feel the need for a nap; I don't always either. The point is our retirement years often give us the luxury of deciding more than we could in our working years about how we spend our time. As followers of Christ, we should want obedience in every area of life, including the area of rest.

The title of this chapter is "The Sacrament of Rest." Is nighttime sleep, a daytime nap, or resting for a spell in a recliner a sacrament? Not in the technical use of the word. We in the Protestant tradition have two sacraments—baptism and communion. Sleep is not on that short list. However, sleep is sacramental in another sense.

A sacrament is a sign, a symbol, an action, that expresses a spiritual truth. Resting, taking a nap, or getting a good night's sleep can remind us of a spiritual truth we should never forget. That "spiritual truth" is the humbling reality we're not indispensable.

When we rest, take a nap, or sleep for the night, we relinquish any control over the world around us. We're reminded everything will go on without us. We're not the center of the universe nor even that small part of the universe within our proximity. Rest is humbling, positioning us for a closer relationship with God. In this way, rest is sacramental, reminding us of our place in God's kingdom.

As we've already noted, Jesus rested in a storm-tossed boat. He also invited his disciples to rest. The gospel writer Mark describes a time when life became hectic for Jesus's disciples and his response was an invitation. "Then, because so many people were coming and going that they did not have a chance to eat, he said to them, 'Come with me by yourselves to a quiet place and get some rest'" (Mark 6:31).

Our comfortableness with rest is a testimony to those around us, who are caught up with people to see, places to go, and things to do. In their rushing here, there, and back again, we might give them pause to see the need for counterbalance in their rushed lives. Our example can be an invitation for them to consider slowing their lives, possibly finding some additional rest.

God told the people of Israel through the prophet Isaiah, "In repentance and rest is your salvation, in quietness and trust is your strength" (Isaiah 30:15). God's people were tempted to put their trust in Egypt for their defense. This is not unlike us when we think that effort and manipulation can make things turn out right. They were not to trust in their own efforts, but in God, resting in him. The same is true for us. The final part of the verse states, sadly, that they didn't follow the Lord's direction on this. "But you would have none of it" (Isaiah 30:15). We can learn from their mistake. In these, our later years, we can practice "repentance," as Isaiah put it, from trying to rush about with great effort to make things right. Instead, we put our trust in God, finding rest in Him.

As we grow older, we find weakness and tiredness more frequent companions. Fortunately, it can also be a time for learning much about the great blessing of rest, a sacramental-like reminder that "in quietness and trust is your strength."

MANAGING THE MEMORY—DAY 18

Following is one of the most familiar jokes about aging. The minister suggests to an elderly parishioner that at her age, she should give serious thought about the hereafter. "Oh, I do," she replies. "When I go into a room or open a drawer, I often ask myself, 'What am I here after?'"

If the joke doesn't sound familiar, then you might have forgotten you heard it. Just kidding.

Age-related forgetfulness often isn't a laughing matter but a real concern as we grow older.

First some encouragement. You're doing quite well in the memory area if you remember you have this small volume titled *Growing Older Gracefully* in your possession and pick it up regularly to read the next chapter.

Okay, I might not have alleviated your concern about memory loss that can come with the aging process. The fact is age-related forgetfulness is a reality, though not the same as Alzheimer's or other kinds of dementia. As our brains get older, they might function a bit more slowly, and we possibly forget a few more details than in earlier years.

The good news is most of us will not lose our accumulated knowledge and wisdom. We can draw upon a lifetime of experiences and faith. The psalmist declared, "I will remember the deeds of the Lord" (Psalm 77:11). David wrote in one of his psalms that we referenced earlier, "Praise the Lord, my soul, and forget not all his benefits" (Psalm 103:2).

In some ways, remembering is a choice. We can, as the psalmists wrote, remember or forget the benefits we've received from God over the years. Pastor and author Tim Keller, in his book *Prayer,* fleshes out the costs resulting from forgetting God's benefits which the psalmist references. Keller writes, "The 'benefits' David lists are those of salvation—the forgiveness of sins; the reception of grace; and the infinite, unconditional love of God."

Keller goes on to observe, "When I forget I am justified by faith alone—I give place to guilt and regret about the past. I therefore live in bondage to idols of power and money that make me feel better about myself. When I forget I'm being sanctified through the presence of God's Holy Spirit—I give up on myself, stop trying to change. When I forget the hope of my future resurrection—I become afraid of aging and death. When I forget my adoption into the family of God—I become full of fears. I don't pray with candor. I lose my confidence. I try to hide my faults from God and myself."[13]

We don't need a perfect memory to remember the benefits God provides.

We can manage our memories because we have a choice as we go through our senior years, the same choice we've had leading to the senior years. That choice is focusing on either the positive or the negative. My experience has been, when I focus on the positive aspects of the past rather than the negative, I find myself remembering the good times and being more forgetful of the bad times.

Whether we express ourselves in grumbling or in gratitude is a choice. Grumbling might not seem like a big deal, but it is—being identified in the Bible as sin. The adult Israelites who were led miraculously out of Egypt never made it into the promised land but died during the forty-year journey. Why? God was punishing them for grumbling. "In this wilderness your bodies will fall—every one of you twenty years old or more who was counted in the census and who has grumbled against me" (Numbers 14:29). Flip to the other end of the Bible, and you have this admonition of the apostle Paul: "Do everything without grumbling" (Philippians 2:14).

If we don't want to be known as "that old grump," then we should resist the temptation to grumble, for a grump, by definition, grumbles. Dwelling on what didn't go well in life keeps the disappointment or failure in the forefront of our memory. On the other hand, focusing on the blessings of the past helps them stick in the memory. What do we want to remember most, the bad or the good?

We who are in our senior years could experience some memory loss, but it's often short-term memory rather than long-term memory that suffers. We might not remember what we had for lunch yesterday, but we have fond memories of meals from long ago, including the favorite dish our mother or grandmother made. Our intact long-term memory means we have a rich history of the Lord's presence and his work in our lives in the past upon which we can reflect in the present.

God's people were told to remember the good God had done for them, "Only be careful, and watch yourselves closely so that you do not forget the things your eyes have seen or let them fade from your heart as long as you live. Teach them to your children and to their children after them" (Deuteronomy 4:9). By the time we reach our senior years, we have a storehouse of memories about how the

Lord has worked in our life. Opening this storehouse, sharing these memories, and living out the lessons we've learned can be our greatest legacy.

The danger with good long-term memory, however, is we can dwell too much on the past—yes, even the good in the past. Memory can play tricks on us, having us recall the past as the "good ol' days" compared to the days we're living now, which often don't seem so good. Isaiah the prophet spoke on behalf of God to God's people who were in exile. Isaiah referenced the "good ol' days" when God led them out of Egypt and miraculously through the wilderness. But then, Isaiah told them, "Forget the former things; do not dwell on the past. See, I am doing a new thing! Now it springs up; do you not perceive it" (Isaiah 43:18–19)?

We might have most of our life behind us, but we still have today, quite possibly tomorrow, and some days beyond tomorrow. The days we are now living, as challenging as they might be, should be embraced. God wants to do a new thing with us each day. Are we open to something new?

The reality is, when you've lived many years, there is much in the past that wasn't good—mistakes were made, sins committed. There could be many regrets. The good news is when we've accepted Jesus Christ as our savior all our past sins are forgiven. This, again, is where the power of choice comes in. We can choose not to fixate on the bad in the past. In fact, it dishonors God when we hold on to that which he's released through his forgiveness.

The apostle Paul persecuted Christians before his conversion. Following his conversion, he was a super achiever as a follower of Jesus. Yet, Paul's past mistakes before becoming a Christian didn't leave him regretful or his successes after becoming a Christian leave him prideful. Neither the mistakes nor the achievements from his past negatively impacted his present and future. Using the imagery of a runner, Paul wrote, "Brothers and sisters, I do not consider myself yet to have taken hold of it. But one thing I do: Forgetting what is behind and straining toward what is ahead, I press on toward the goal to win the prize for which God has called me heavenward in Christ Jesus" (Philippians 3:13–14).

Our memory might not be what it used to be, and that's okay. We're not held accountable for what we can't help we've forgotten. We're called to use what we do remember for God's glory. By God's grace, we can manage our memories, making the best of today and the tomorrows with which we might be gifted. Now, if we could just remember that.

THE STEWARDSHIP OF THE SENIOR YEARS—DAY 19

"God loves you and has a wonderful plan for your life" was a popular Christian phrase when I was much younger, a phrase containing much truth. I've taken the liberty of adapting the phrase. "God loves you, and others have a wonderful plan for your life." My adaptation is tongue-in-cheek, but also has an element of truth.

Others have expectations of us, and we of them. This is true throughout life, but truer than ever during our working years. Our career or job demands much time and effort. We were paid to show up at work. Those paying us had a right to expect something from us. This was often a large chunk of time, frequently around forty hours a week—plus commuting time. We who are retired have fewer people with expectations on how we spend each day, giving us more discretionary time.

What do we do with the hours that were previously occupied with earning a living now we don't have the obligations our job demanded? Who shall we call, text, or meet for lunch? What shall we read? What hobby or hobbies should we pursue and to what extent? Where and how much should we volunteer our time? Options of how we spend our time often multiply in our retirement years. This new freedom reveals our true character, our real motives.

Retirement can tempt us with the philosophy we've earned the right to do what we want, entertaining ourselves in whatever way we wish. We're tempted in this stage of life as much as any previous stage to grab all the gusto we can.

We can also shift to the other end of the spectrum. Rather than rushing about in pursuit of one entertaining distraction after another, we can decide to take it easy. We've "paid our dues" and feel we've earned the privilege to kick back, doing nothing much at all.

But for the follower of Jesus, retirement doesn't come with a gold card giving us access to a life where we can be self-indulgent—entertaining or pampering ourselves by doing little or nothing. The call of Christ is a continuing carrying of the cross, involving the self-denial he invited us to embrace when we began life's journey with him. The golden years are a golden opportunity for serving him as never before, yielding ourselves to his agenda. Our prayer should be something to the effect, "Lord, what would you have me do, who would you have me meet, what would you have me say?" Gandalf told Frodo in J. R. R. Tolkien's *Lord of the Rings*, "All we have to decide is what to do with the time that is given us."

With the advancing years, we could find opportunities are not as abundant as in earlier years. We no longer are in the mainstream of the river of life with the occasional rapids that made life interesting and exciting but are now in the still backwaters and eddies. This means we must be intentional, even aggressive, at paddling along, looking for new opportunities to live life fully around the next bend in the river.

We don't know how many days we have left on earth, but each day affords us the same sixty minutes in each hour as those younger than us possess. As a disciple of Jesus, we should ask ourselves if we're using the precious time which we have left in the way the Lord wants us to use it. The psalmist declared, yielding before the Lord, "My times are in your hands" (Psalm 31:15).

How should we use this time? Well, we all have God-given talents we've used, developing them over the years. Our current expression of these talents in our later years might or might not have much to do with the skills we needed in the work we did while earning a living. The fact is, we're all gifted with things we can do, be they great or few. We're called to exercise these gifts God has given us in giving ourselves to others. We could even discover new gifts and abilities left dormant previously because earning a living was so demanding.

The Christian concept of stewardship has traditionally included the three "Ts" of time, talent, and treasure. We've looked at the first two: time and talent. What about our treasure?

Here again our circumstances vary greatly. We have less accumulated wealth than some and more than others. No matter the amount, the questions are the same. How much should we spend on ourselves? How much do we share with others? How much do we leave our heirs?

J. Oswald Sanders is reported to have said, "The basic question is not how much of our money we should give to God, but how much of God's money we should keep for ourselves." Christ's call to give ourselves over to him is a call that includes putting our finances under his lordship. Yes, we should be good stewards of our treasure, whether small or great.

Years ago, I added a fourth "T" to the three familiar "Ts" of time, talent, and treasure. That fourth "T" of stewardship is trouble. Are we good stewards of our troubles, of our pain? Moving through our senior years, we can't escape the troubles or pain that come with aging. How will we handle them?

Well-known minister and writer Frederick Buechner shared with a small group a portion of some fiction he had written. His listeners realized, though fictional, the story revealed the deep hurt Buechner himself had experienced being raised in a home with an alcoholic and abusive father. After the reading, a man in the group came up to him, deeply moved, and told Buechner, "You have a good deal of pain in your life, and you have been a good steward of it."[14]

What does that mean, that we can be a good steward of our troubles or pain? First, troubles can drive us to God. Looking back on my ministry, I don't recall a single person who started attending church, stating as the reason, "Life is going so well for me I want a closer connection with God who has blessed me so." To the contrary, countless people showed up for the first time at church, sharing with me, "Something terrible has happened in my life, and I need God."

Second, troubles can make us a better person rather than a bitter person—the choice is ours. I have known many people who have had multiple serious troubles in their lives and yet, despite all the pain, were beautiful, joyful, enthusiastic, and gracious.

Third, troubles God has helped us cope and deal with give us the compassion and resources necessary for coming alongside others, helping them go through similar troubles. Our troubled past can be helpful to someone's troubled present.

Being good stewards of our troubles pays off in the end. The palmist prayed, "Though you have made me see troubles, many and bitter, you will restore my life again; from the depths of the earth you will again bring me up" (Psalm 71:20).

Good stewardship in our senior years means we handle our time, talent, treasure, and even our troubles in a way that will bring glory to God. Good stewardship also means we are still in a position in our last years for bringing God's good to the people he's placed around us.

GRACE AND GRATITUDE—DAY 20

A great antidote for keeping us from becoming grumpy older people is practicing gratitude. We've addressed the subject of gratitude before, but its importance deserves more emphasis. Establishing the habit of being thankful is good for any age group, but the habit yields maximum dividends as we navigate the senior years. In our senior years, we find ourselves having to let go of much. In many ways, our senior years are the declining years. Now, more than ever, we should adopt an attitude of gratitude, focusing more on what we still have rather than on what we no longer have, and what we've gained that we didn't have before. We can't express gratitude while grumbling at the same time. Like oil and water, they don't mix.

Gratitude is learned—we don't come by the attribute naturally. We often must remind children when they've received a gift, "Now, what do you say?" Though by our elder years, we've hopefully learned the importance of giving thanks—this is the time when we should up our game of gratitude. If we don't watch ourselves, grumbling will come easier in these later years with declining health, a growing list of lost loved ones, a widening disconnect with a fast-changing world, and shrinking opportunities.

We need an ongoing refresher course on gratitude. The best textbook on gratitude is the Bible. Thirteen times in the Psalms, for instance, the psalmist declares, "Give thanks to the Lord."

What's tricky is we can have a belief in God but lack gratitude. The apostle Paul wrote, "For although they knew God, they neither glorified him as God nor gave thanks to him, but their thinking became futile and their foolish hearts were darkened" (Romans 1:21).

Paul is likely referencing non-Christians, people who have only a general belief in God. But the fact Paul dovetails unbelief and ingratitude should put us on notice concerning the importance of embracing gratitude as Christ followers.

There's a natural correlation between being a Christian and being grateful, which we should embrace. Being a Christian means receiving God's grace. Grace is a gift—an undeserved favor. We have God's gift of forgiveness through Jesus. What should we say when we receive a gift? Thank you.

God offers forgiveness through his gracious act of going to the cross, paying the price, and accepting the penalty for our sin. The apostle Paul wrote, "Thanks be to God, who delivers me through Jesus Christ our Lord!" (Romans 7:25). Our life with Christ should be steeped in gratitude because his grace was so wonderfully expressed toward us. God's grace and our gratitude go together. No matter how our life plays out as we grow older, we can deepen our understanding of God's gracious acts toward us. We are his now and forever.

I find gratitude occupies a bigger part of my overall attitude when I'm intentional about frequently practicing thanksgiving. For instance, sometimes I spend my entire quiet time, my daily devotional time, in nothing but giving thanks. Usually, I do so chronologically, beginning with my childhood, expressing gratitude for the benefits and blessings that were part of my growing up years. I then move on to early adulthood, then middle age, and, finally, the current senior years. Sure, there are events in the past that weren't good, but there were also aspects in the past that were. I focus on these, giving thanks. Sometimes, I randomize my reasons for which I should be thankful. After such a prayer time, I can't help but feel better. What I find is intentionally practicing gratitude reduces my tendency to become a grumpy old person.

There are always things which prove difficult, if not impossible, for which to give thanks. Perhaps it's financial difficulties, an illness or disease, a hurt or alienated relationship, or the negative ramifications in general with getting older. Let me make two affirmations about the reality of brokenness in our lives, particularly now in our later years.

First, the negatives can distract us from seeing the positives. I sometimes use the example of taking a sheet of paper and putting several dots on the page. I then hold up the paper, asking someone what they see. Invariably they respond, "I see some dots." I then remind them this is true, but the main thing they see is white paper. The dots only take up a small portion of the paper. It's easy to let the things that are wrong and bad distract us from identifying the many things that are right and good. For instance, we grumble about needing help from others, but how about being grateful we do receive help from others?

The second affirmation is the bad we experience is meant by God to bring about some ultimate good, and he is with us, making that happen. We must remember God is always with us. King David said in his famous psalm, "Even though I walk through the darkest valley, I will fear no evil, for you are with me" (Psalm 23:4). God didn't keep David from going through the dark valley, but God was with him when he did so. My mother lived alone a portion of her last years. My sister offered to come and get Mom, so she could spend Thanksgiving Day with my sister and her family. My mother declined the offer saying, "I won't be alone. The Lord will be with me."

Philip Yancey writes in *Vanishing Grace*, "Like an iPod listener dancing in a subway station full of glum commuters, a Christian hears a different sound, one of joy and laughter, on the other side of pain and death."[15]

Whatever good we don't have in our older age, and whatever bad we do have in our later years, what's most important is we have the Lord. The apostle Paul, after writing about the final enemy we face, calling this enemy the "sting of death," declares, "But thanks be to God. He gives us the victory through our Lord Jesus Christ" (1 Corinthians 15:57). Yes, Christ is for us, reason enough—the best reason—to give thanks. Always!

GRIEVING LOSSES—DAY 21

Grieving frequently increases as we age. We grieve over many losses. There's the loss of loved ones. We attend more funerals in our older age. For some, there's the life-changing loss of a mate. We grieve over loss of health and/or mobility. We grieve over the good times in the past—that they're in the past. We grieve over the bad times, including the hurt from others. We grieve over the negative circumstances that were beyond our control, robbing us of what we believe could have been. We grieve over our past mistakes and sins, realizing often we were our own worst enemy. We grieve.

How can we handle the grief as we look back on our lives? How does God want us dealing with our grief? How can he help us do so?

First, remembering how God comes alongside us in our grief can prove helpful. David wrote, "You have kept count of my tossings; put my tears in your bottle. Are they not in your book?" (Psalm 56:8 ESV).

Though David's grief was caused by his Philistine enemies, God is no less concerned for what grieves us, no matter the source. Our tears stored in his bottle, our grief notated in his book: both are images that communicate God's empathy, God's care for us.

Grieving over the death of those with whom we've been close is painful. With funerals and memorial services proliferating during our senior years, we can feel like the sole survivor. How should we view this attrition by death? As a pastor, I've presided over many funerals. I realized early on that grieving the loss of someone we care about can be a good grief. At many services, I've shared Alfred, Lord Tennyson's sentiment, "It's better to have loved and lost than never to have loved at all." Our grief can be a sign, albeit a painful one, that we had something good going with the person for which we can give thanks. The grieving over their absence from us can be wrapped in gratitude for how much value they added to our life when they were with us. Such gratitude can help with our grief.

Grieving over the loss of health or mobility is grieving over the shrinking boundaries concerning our daily activity. We'd rather stay healthy and keep on moving, but that's not normally how the aging process works. In our older age, we're old enough to know better.

As disciples of Jesus, we can be assured his plans for us can be carried out with declining health and increasingly limited mobility. He knew we would face such limitations, and he has a plan. As pastor, I often visited our shut-ins, frequently reminding them that one thing, for sure, which they could still do was pray, pray for me their pastor, pray for their church, and pray for others. No matter what we lose concerning our health and mobility, there's still always something God has for us to do.

Grieving over the good times in our past, that they are no more, can distract us from whatever good he has for us in the present. Replacing grief over the good ol' days with gratitude for them will put us in a better mental position for seeing the good in the present. "I will give thanks to you, Lord, with all my heart; I will tell of all your wonderful deeds" (Psalm 9:1).

Grieving over how someone hurt us in the past only continues to pull that pain into the present, dragging the hurt into whatever future here on earth remains for us. We should bury this grieving before we are buried. Why should we let someone from years ago continue inflicting pain upon us in our old age, someone who, more than likely, is dead? We aren't as strong as we used to be, unable to carry as much as we grow older, so something we should stop carrying is a grudge—an unnecessary burden. God's Word frequently reminds us forgive. Jesus instructs us to pray in what we call the Lord's Prayer, "Forgive us our sins as we forgive those who sin against us." Rejoicing over God's forgiveness of our sins should prompt our forgiving others. We can move beyond the grief that comes with carrying a grudge.

Grieving over how circumstances dealt us a nasty blow can leave us a bitter old person. "If only that had turned out differently." "I wish that hadn't happened." The reality is we don't have the power to *change* the past, but we do have the power, with the Lord's help, to change how we *view* the past. Joseph, in the Old Testament, had been sold into slavery by his brothers. Eventually, through some amazing circumstances, Joseph oversaw the food distribution in Egypt during a great famine. Joseph's brothers came to Egypt in a desperate effort to get food for their families, not knowing their brother oversaw the government program. When they found out, they were shocked and fearful of retaliation from Joseph. Joseph reassured them, "But God sent me ahead of you to preserve for you a remnant on earth and to save your lives by a great deliverance" (Genesis 45:7). Joseph saw, both in his brothers' nasty treatment of himself, and the many difficult circumstances he endured following their betrayal, God was at work through it all. God also was at work through our own painful past.

Grieving over our own past mistakes and sins is unnecessary. When we have Christ as our Savior all is forgiven. The psalmist declared, "As far as the east is from the west, so far has he removed our transgressions from us" (Psalm 103:12). The psalmist didn't use north and south, which have limits; you can only go so far north or south before north becomes south, and south becomes north. Go east or west and you keep on going east or west, with no end in sight, infinity. If God casts away our sins an infinite distance, then how dare we keep holding them near with the grip of regret?

Yes, our griefs can come in many forms in our senior years, a golden opportunity in the golden years for drawing closer to God, who can help us with our griefs. "But you, God, see the trouble of the afflicted; you consider their grief and take it in hand" (Psalm 10:14).

SELF-FORGETFULNESS—DAY 22

Aging can provide a greater comfort with self because we don't have as much to prove. This doesn't always mean we're never tempted to be centered on self. This tendency toward being self-centered is present in every age bracket. Throughout our lives, at every stage of life, when most of us look at a group photo in which we're a member, we first look for ourselves in the photo. However, the aging process can accentuate this tendency toward self-centeredness. Growing older can result in fixating on our ailments, our lack of mobility, what we failed to accomplish, and the feeling the world is passing us by, leaving us in the dust to which we're soon destined to return. Feeling sorry for oneself is easy.

Growing older is also a time when we can be jealous or envious of what our elderly peers have that we don't have, further drawing attention to ourselves. R. Paul Stevens writes, "An aging person can experience envy of another's near-perfect health, near-perfect family (and what family does not have problems, though some seem to be blighted with catastrophic misfortunes?), or amazing financial resources to enjoy retirement while he or she ekes out a frugal existence until death."[16]

Growing older can also result in our world growing smaller, tempting the adoption of the perspective where we're the center of our small world. This mini world is far from perfect, making a pity party of one a reality.

As a pastor, I sometimes had lay leaders make announcements or share something before the congregation or a smaller group of congregants. Many were self-conscious when speaking before others, muddling through with less than good results. I encouraged them to focus on those listening—with a desire to give them important information. When they could forget about themselves, they did a better job communicating.

We might not speak before a group, but we could find ourselves entering a room where people are present. We can have a better experience when entering a room filled with people if, rather than focusing on ourselves—wondering if anyone will talk to us—we search out someone who looks like they're thinking the same thing. We never end up being a wallflower, if we look for a wallflower with whom we can start a conversation. The result is the other person no longer feels like a wallflower either.

While making our way through our senior years, how can we keep from putting the focus on self? How about this approach?

If the senior years are a time when we have a greater tendency to be forgetful, then let's channel that tendency into a healthy self-forgetfulness. Timothy Keller wrote a small book titled *The Freedom of Self-Forgetfulness*. Keller references 1 Corinthians 3:21–4:7, writing, "Paul is saying that he has reached a place where his ego draws no more attention to itself than any other part of his body. He has reached a place where he is not thinking about himself anymore."[17] What a great place to arrive.

If we've been growing in Christ as we grow older, then we have more of Christ in us and less of us in us. Our model should be the aging apostle Paul, who wrote, "I no longer live, but Christ lives in me" (Galatians 2:20). John Newton wrote in a letter, "By nature, SELF rules in the heart. When this idol is brought low, and we are willing to be the Lord's, and to apply to Him for strength and direction, that we may serve Him—the good work is begun."[18]

As Christians our ego is not on the throne of our being, but Christ is. Our fixation is on him, not on self, because of what he has done for us in the past, who he is for us in the present, and where he is taking us in the future—home to his heaven. Even with the often-increasing level of aches and pains that come with aging, we're not a grumpy old man or woman, but a glorious elder person to those around us because Christ dwells within us.

This results in what Keller calls gospel-humility. We're humbled, particularly by what Christ has done for us in being our Savior. Keller then applies this gospel-humility to our interpersonal relationships. "The thing we would remember from meeting a truly gospel-humble person is how much they seemed to be totally interested in us. Because the essence of gospel-humility is not thinking more of myself or thinking less of myself, it is thinking of myself less."[19] Keller then fleshes out what this means, "I stop connecting every experience, every conversation, with myself. In fact, I stop thinking about myself. The freedom of self-forgetfulness."[20]

A growing presence of Christ within us can make us a more likable person, someone with whom people enjoy spending time. When others meet us or come for a visit, they should walk away less impressed with us and more impressed with themselves.

We can start now, focusing our conversations with others on them, not us. Here are some guidelines I find helpful.

1. Early in the conversation ask the person how they're doing.
2. Practice active listening, which means listening and not thinking about what we will say when it's our turn to talk.
3. Ask a follow-up question, which will come to us rather easily, if we're practicing active listening.
4. Make eye contact.
5. Resist "topping" the other person's story with one from a myriad of stories from our own past.
6. Ask the person how you can pray for them.
7. Look for a way to encourage the person.
8. Express gratitude for the conversation and, when applicable, for their visit or offer of help.

Being forgetful can happen more frequently as we grow older. Let's put a positive spin on it. By being self-forgetful, we're doing our part to cancel out the caricature of old people always talking about themselves.

POSSESSING PEACE—DAY 23

"If you can keep your head when everybody around you is losing his, then it is very probable that you don't understand the situation." This maxim has been around for about a hundred years, and for good reason—we resonate with the thought, especially those of us in our senior years.

We often feel we have reason enough for being worried and anxious at our age. A person would be clueless if not worried, right? That's how we're often tempted to feel.

When I was younger, I wondered why older people worried so much—that as they got older, they appeared to worry more. This was illogical in my estimation because, of all people, they should have learned worrying doesn't help any situation, might make it worse and, at the very least, makes a person more miserable.

Now that I'm older myself, I see things differently. I still worry and can be anxious. Peace-robbing thoughts infiltrate my thinking. Doing some research, I accumulated a list of common fears which prompt worry and anxiety in older people.

1. Loss of independence
2. Memory loss

3. Declining health
4. Running short on money
5. Safety and security issues
6. Not being able to live at home
7. Death of a spouse or other loved one
8. Falling and getting hurt
9. Not being able to drive
10. Inability to manage daily activities
11. Loss of personal dignity
12. Isolation or loneliness

When I shared this list with my wife, she commented that a major source of anxiety was missing. That's worrying about our adult children and our grandchildren. When our two children were young, we could kiss their scrapes, apply a bandage, and make the owie all better. Not so now. We watch both our children and our grandchildren go through tough times, realizing there's little we can do about it.

Every stage of life provides worrisome situations, but there are unique circumstances we seniors face, which can prompt us to worry and be anxious. So, what can we do to manage worry and anxiety in our senior years and, instead, possess a higher degree of peace?

The reality is removing or even significantly managing any of the above-itemized circumstances in our elder years isn't going to happen. If we can't do much about controlling them, then can we control how we'll respond to them? How, then, can we possess peace in the face of that which is not inherently peace-producing, but the very opposite—worrisome and anxiety-producing?

Because the reflections on aging in this book are unabashedly biblical, let me share a wonderful verse in the Bible from the inspired prophet Isaiah. "You will keep in perfect peace those whose minds are steadfast, because they trust in you" (Isaiah 26:3). God giving us his perfect peace in our later years will require a steadfast trust in him, according to this statement from his Word.

One of my favorite photographs is of a lighthouse being pummeled by huge waves. The lighthouse keeper stands in the lighthouse doorway. The picture was taken in 1989 by French photographer Jean Guichard from a helicopter. The lighthouse keeper heard the helicopter from within the lighthouse and thought he was being rescued. That's when he opened the door and stepped out. When he realized he was not being rescued, he went back into the lighthouse, closing the door behind him, but not before the photographer caught the amazing image. The image is powerful, showing a person who is safe amid a raging storm in a lighthouse firmly grounded on an island of rock. This is a stormy picture, but also a picture which portrays peace.

The psalmist David declared, "Yes, my soul, find rest in God; my hope comes from him. Truly he is my rock and my salvation; he is my fortress, I will not be shaken" (Psalm 62:5–6). We now live in the post-New Testament times, so in the unique storms that lash seniors, we can find our firm footing in a faith based on our Rock who is Jesus.

Reflect with me on the time Jesus invited his disciples to get in a boat with him and cross to the other side of the lake. During the journey, Jesus fell asleep in the boat, then a tremendous storm came up. We read, "The disciples [including Peter] woke him and said to him, 'Teacher, don't you care if we drown?'" Jesus got up and miraculously calmed the storm. He then asked them, "Why are you so afraid? Do you still have no faith" (Mark 4:38, 40)?

The disciples had faith enough that Jesus could save them, that's why they woke him. What they lacked was a trust in his care for them. "Teacher, don't you care if we drown?" I have found situations where I'm tempted to worry, even after I've brought the issue before the Lord. I have little doubt he has the power to deal with what's worrying me, nor do I doubt his wisdom for doing what is right. What I struggle with is having the confidence that he cares. The first time I identified this as the issue was during a crisis with a grandchild. I found myself harboring the unspoken question the disciples shouted at Jesus over the roar of the storm, "Don't you care?"

He does care. He calmed the storm for the disciples. He can calm our storms, too, or at least stay with us through the storms. Years after the incident in the storm-tossed boat, Peter wrote some Christians on how Jesus could address their fears. "Cast all your anxiety on him because he cares for you" (1 Peter 5:7).

We're to do this too—cast the anxieties we face in our later years upon Jesus because he cares for us. Because of him, and the fact that he cares, we can possess peace.

EMBRACE THE ORDINARY DAY— DAY 24

Ordinary days can be wonderful days. I'm reminded of this when I watch a news report showing people struggling with the aftermath of a flood, fire, tornado, hurricane, or some other natural disaster. I'm reminded how valuable ordinary days are when I hear of a friend who received a bad report from the doctor. The list is endless of how a day can turn to anything but ordinary. That's why ordinary days are so wonderful. God must love ordinary days, because he's made so many of them.

We who are in the later years of life often find ourselves facing more ordinary days than when we were younger. Back then, we dealt with the unscheduled events involving young children getting scraped knees and teenagers with an old car that broke down, leaving them stranded and in need of rescuing. Our job often threw surprises our way that demanded immediate, often creative responses. Now much of the fast-paced life is behind us. Our life is more frequently represented by a quiet routine that doesn't vary as much from day to day as in the past.

This more relaxed schedule can result in boredom, perhaps even depression. We're not as busy. There's not as much to look forward to. How are we going to respond to these new developments? If at this stage of life, we have many ordinary days, we should make the most of them.

An enlightening verse is Psalm 118:24. "This is the day that the Lord has made; let us rejoice and be glad in it" (ESV). The psalmist had described in an earlier verse how life's not perfect. "The Lord has disciplined me severely" (v. 18). We can identify. The senior years have their unique challenges. Yet, throughout the psalm, the writer affirms the presence and help of the Lord. "The Lord is my strength and my song; he has become my salvation" (v. 14). If we're the Lord's person, having him as our Savior and Lord, this is true for us as well. God is at work, so the psalmist can declare, "This is the day that the Lord has made; let us rejoice and be glad in it." We, too, can rejoice in each day, including ordinary days.

Each day is a gift from God, but we can neglect the gift of today and fixate on days in the past, either with regret or nostalgia. We can also fixate on the future, either with anticipation, or with fear and anxiety.

A gift should be appreciated. How would we feel if, upon giving a birthday gift to someone, the person responds, "But I like what you gave me last year better," or "How about next year you get me ...?" We'd want the recipient to appreciate the gift we gave them now. Today is the day with which God has gifted us. We should find reasons to rejoice and be glad in it.

The apostle Paul admonishes us to "rejoice in the Lord always. I will say it again: Rejoice!" (Philippians 4:4). That means finding reasons for rejoicing every day, no matter what that day holds, including all those ordinary days. Marilyn McEntyre writes, "I know that part of what will be given me in this time is a chance to practice gratitude."[21]

This practice of identifying reasons for being thankful not only shows appreciation to God for his blessings, but also helps us identify the many things that are good in each day. R. Paul Stevens writes, "Thanksgiving drives away discontentment."[22] We don't have to be discontented with ordinary days but can embrace them.

Bible commentator from a past era, Matthew Henry, wrote, "In all conditions of life it is our wisdom and duty to make the best of that which is and not to throw away the comfort of what we could have because we have not all we would have."[23]

The reality is ordinary days afford plenty of opportunities for being thankful and rejoicing. We don't have to wait for extraordinary days involving celebration or happy surprises, which are often few and far between. Charles Cummings, a Trappist monk, wrote, "We put religious experience too easily into the category of the unusual, and never expect to find God in the flow of the usual things we do. The rich, spiritual dimension of our ordinary activities is thus lost to us."[24]

Our senior years put us in a better position to stop and smell the roses. Unlike in years past when our view of blessings was blurred by rushing, we can, with the slower pace in the senior years, see in better focus the blessings we have, savoring the good God has put around us.

We must be intentional about embracing each rather ordinary day. We don't come by the practice naturally. Along with stopping to smell the roses, we can focus our gaze on something interesting outside our window, especially if the roses aren't in bloom. Install a bird feeder just beyond the window. Look through the window at something more distant, perhaps at the wind waving the tree branches or slowly pushing the clouds across our window's view. Bring nature indoors, purchasing a flower that has buds, promising blossoms we can anticipate.

Savor that cup of coffee or tea cupped in our hands while giving thanks to the Lord for the beverage and other blessings that come to mind. Be grateful for the rest God gives as we take a nap. Determine to call, message, email, or in some other way connect with one or two people each day, thus maintaining a significant sphere of influence, counteracting the entropy of growing isolation that can come with growing older.

Every day God has us on earth means he has a plan for us for each of those days, as ordinary as they might seem. Each day is a gift. Unwrapping the goodness which he has for us in each day is our responsibility. Let's affirm with the psalmist, "This is the day that the Lord has made; let us rejoice and be glad in it."

BE OPEN TO CHANGE—DAY 25

Growing older brings on a whole new set of changes. Many are unwanted changes.

1. Feeling useless and unproductive
2. Experiencing grief through losing a mate, siblings, or friends
3. A slow but certain ebbing of health or strength
4. A serious health condition developing
5. Loss of freedom with having to give up driving
6. Living arrangement changes, often resulting in a loss of independence.

No one, of any age, likes change, even babies don't like being changed. However, the Greek philosopher Heraclitus reminds us that "there is nothing permanent except change."

I recall the story of a man bragging about the antique ax he owned, "This ax belonged to my great-great-grandfather. The handle has been replaced two or three times and the head has been replaced at least once, but other than that, it's the same ax my great-great-grandfather owned." Really? Everything changed about the ax. Change is inevitable.

A tree that doesn't bend in the wind will break in the wind. Even window glass flexes slightly, otherwise the window would more easily shatter. Unless we're intentional about remaining flexible as we age, we're not going to adapt in a good way to the changes often imposed on us.

I recall my mother, sometime in the last years of her life, reflecting on the day, years earlier, when she and Dad gave up their car. They watched out the living room window as my sister and her husband, who had purchased the car from them, backed out of the driveway and drove off. This was a major change for my parents, losing a significant amount of their mobility. But Mom and Dad adjusted to this change, due in large measure, I believe, to their faith.

We who have faith in the Lord are in a good place, because faith can make us flexible. When we put our trust in God, we're opening ourselves to him, to his setting the agenda for the remaining time he has for us here on earth, though that agenda is not always what we would choose. Marilyn McEntyre writes, "What helps me most, when I can do it, is to relax into God's hands and relinquish all effort to make things different from what they are."[25]

As we navigate through the senior years, we experience not only outward but inward changes. I find, for instance, I no longer enjoy selling my photography on a stock photo web site. For years, I delighted in having the images accepted by the website and watching the purchases of the different images tally up. Admittedly the process has gotten more complicated over the years, but the main reason I no longer pursue selling my photography is I've lost interest in doing so. And that's okay. "Been there, done that" is the phrase that's applicable. Now I'm satisfied with sharing my photography on social media with friends and acquaintances.

Diann and I enjoyed camping with our small camper trailer. We finally were honest with each other, admitting camping had become hard work. We also were no longer comfortable towing a trailer down the road. Selling the camper trailer prompted mixed feelings for both of us. There was sadness with the camping era coming to an end, but selling the trailer also came with relief.

A good way to face the inevitable changes that come with aging is being intentional about identifying the positives in the changes. I posted a photo on Facebook of my hand, showing a purple bruise. I wrote we often see statements that start "you know you're getting older when ..." I wrote I could add another to that list. "You know you're getting older when you notice a bruise and don't know how you got it." Many older Facebook friends responded, expressing their similar experience.

Facebook friend Patty posted this wonderful response, also agreeing with my observation. "Yes, I sure do. Now when I look down at my hands, I immediately see how my hands have morphed into my mother's hands. Rather than focus on the wrinkled skin and age spots, I turn my attention to how blessed I am to have good working hands, and I fondly remember how much my mom did with her hands to help others until she was just shy of ninety-five years of age. Blessings abound with age too." Patty, when she looks at her aging hands, rather than lamenting, experiences a closeness to her mother, focusing on the blessings of aging. That's a positive response to what most would see as a negative change.

We might grumble at the changes coming our way in our senior years, but we can't change the fact change is inevitable. We can only change how we respond to change.

Proverbs 19:23 states, "The fear of the Lord leads to life; then one rests content, untouched by trouble." The troubling changes of growing older don't have to rob us of being content. A "fear of the Lord" is a respectful trust in him and his ways, bringing a contentment that defies explanation.

The apostle Paul wrote concerning this in his letter to the Corinthian Christians while he was imprisoned for his faith. "I have learned to be content whatever the circumstances. I know what it is to be in need, and I know what it is to have plenty. I have learned the secret of being content in any and every situation, whether well fed or hungry, whether living in plenty or in want. I can do all this through him who gives me strength" (Philippians 4:11–13).

Contentment was something Paul said he learned. We've learned a lot by the time we're in our senior years, but we still have more we can learn. We can learn, through Jesus's strength, to be content in the face of change.

REDEFINING RETIREMENT—DAY 26

The word "retirement" is not found in the Bible—neither should the word be in the vocabulary of the person who is serious about being God's person in the senior years. Okay, so we can't get away from the word. On many forms, I find myself having to check the "retired" box, which is the category that fits best. Yes, I will tell someone, "I'm retired," but I frequently qualify that, if the person gives me the opportunity.

Author John Piper wrote, "Don't throw your life away on the American dream of retirement."[26] Secular society and our culture promotes ideas concerning retirement that run counter to what God calls our lives to look like in our senior years. Think about the images you've seen portraying seniors in their retirement years—likely they're images of playing golf, sitting around a table at a luxurious retirement facility, playing cards, lounging on a cruise ship, or playing shuffle board. There's nothing wrong with these activities, but such images often project an ideal retirement which focuses on self, a view which followers of Christ shouldn't subscribe. God's call is for something more than a life of leisure and self-pampering after retirement.

R. Paul Stevens wrote, "There is work after work!"[27] Stevens expands on this call from God to work after work, "My calling is to empower the whole people of God for service in the world, and to care for and love God, my family, and my neighbor, and to make beautiful things to embellish the earth and people. That calling has remained constant even though the manifestation of the calling has changed radically. And now, at 78, I am still trying to find out what I am to do with my life when I finally grow up!"[28]

We're to move beyond seeing retirement as a time for pampering ourselves, enjoying the fruits of our labors, spending on ourselves, and entertaining ourselves to death. Redefining retirement and conforming to a lifestyle that reflects God's purposes is his plan for us.

This calling from God in our senior years will look different for each of us, just as our lives looked different from others during our working years. For my wife and me, our senior years mean living in two different locations—two different countries—the United States and Mexico, so we can be near our daughter and her family (in Mexico) and our son and his family (in Florida). Our daughter started a mission in Mexico, and our son helped plant a church in Florida. We see a significant part of our call from God at this stage in our lives as a coming alongside our two adult children, supporting God's call on their lives.

Some might find ways for being God's conduit of his goodness through volunteering with an organization or ministry. Others will find physical limitations directing them toward a ministry of prayer or of listening, ministries that don't require mobility or healthy bodies. The opportunities for living out God's call in our senior years are many and varied.

The psalmist said concerning the righteous, "They will still bear fruit in old age, they will stay fresh and green" (Psalm 92:14). The righteous are those who are right with God. When we're right with God, we find ourselves in the center of God's will, being productive, fresh and green in our old age. Our work in the "retirement" years most often won't involve earning money (though for some, by necessity or by choice, it will). Our work also might not involve producing a product or providing a service the way it did when we were earning a living (though, again, for some it might).

Retiring from a paying job is not the end of our working life—the work just changes. Every ending affords the opportunity for a new beginning.

During our paid working years, we were limited in what we could do because much of our time was consumed doing that for which we would get paid. After the work-for-pay years, the options are much more plentiful.

We could face the temptation of being slothful or lazy with greater severity in our "retirement" years than when working at a job. No one's telling us what to do. Even if we were self-employed during our earning years, the need for income was a strong motivation for working. Now, after the paid job is behind us, we must be self-motivated. Though we can enjoy a slower pace, we still must keep moving in some way, being fruitful for the Lord.

Redefining retirement that conforms to Christ's will for us requires reflection on our part. R. Paul Stevens stated, "The questions raised by retirement can become the most important self-assessment tools for the rest of your life: What have I done with my life up to now? What contribution to family, neighbor, to the world, and the environment do I still want to make? What is the meaning of life? What am I living for? What is most important in my life?"[29]

No longer restricted by the demands or obligations that come with a job, we find ourselves in a position where we can decide how to spend our time. This newfound freedom of choice reveals our true nature, interests, passions, and priorities.

We could also find ourselves not deciding much at all, letting ourselves coast through our remaining days with no rhyme or reason for our continued existence. This is not good. Being intentional about how we live out our final years is the way to redefine our retirement.

We often ask children, "What do you want to be when you grow up?" We should ask ourselves much the same question, "What do I want to be as I grow older?"

FINISHING WELL—DAY 27

Our grandson is a runner, so there's no surprise we've been at many of his races. I've noticed most everyone starts the race well. When the starting gun goes off, there's no way to identify who is a fast runner and who isn't, who has endurance and who doesn't. This only becomes apparent at the finish line.

Finishing well is important in almost every enterprise. A novel could begin well, but if the ending doesn't satisfy, the reader finds the story disappointing. In cooking or baking, you can put all the ingredients together as the recipe indicates, but if you end up burning the food, then all is for naught. A woodworking project can go well, but if you mess up the finishing stage with the stain or varnish, the project won't be beautiful. A team can start out the game playing well, getting ahead in the score, but unless they finish well, an upset is likely.

We can recall famous people who accomplished a great deal in their lives, being admired and respected by many, but who messed up their lives in the later years, becoming infamous. What they did wrong near the end of their lives far outshines the good they had done earlier, their legacy tarnished, often badly.

As we navigate the senior years, finishing well should be uppermost in our minds. Those around us are watching how we cope with the aging process, especially those younger than we are. The later years are the litmus test which reveals what we're really like and who we really are. Our deepest convictions and true character are no longer concealed by the blur of busyness. As the aging process slows us, and we slog through the difficulties that can come with this stage of life, who we truly are comes into sharper focus for others. They're watching how we respond to new limitations, cope with health issues, and handle the loss of our peers. Our last chance for leaving a good legacy is how we'll deal with the looming reality of our own death. Will we finish well by dying well?

With the challenges of growing older, do those around us see our fear increasing and faith decreasing, or do they see our fear decreasing and our faith increasing? Aging brings tests unique to our faith. Will these tests make us bitter or better? Will they prompt a drifting from the Lord or drawing closer to the Lord? The process of sanctification (becoming more like Christ) as we grow older can continue, plateau, or even decrease. The choice is ours.

If we feel we've led a far from stellar life up until now, now is not too late, we can still finish well. An example is one of the two criminals crucified alongside Jesus. He reprimanded the other criminal being crucified alongside himself and Jesus for mocking Jesus, admitting that they were getting what they deserved, but Jesus was innocent. This criminal then turned to Jesus, making a request. "Jesus, remember me when you come into your kingdom." Jesus reassured him, "Truly I tell you, today you will be with me in paradise" (Luke 23:42–43). We don't know what this criminal had done to deserve capital punishment, but whatever his offense was, Jesus offered him forgiveness and eternal life. The man finished well.

A name given Satan is "Accuser" meaning he accuses us of sin which has been forgiven, sin for which we are no longer held accountable—once we've accepted Christ as our Savior. Satan wants us believing we are unworthy of God's acceptance. Reminiscing about our past can leave us feeling like a failure resulting from our sins of commission, the bad that we did, and sins of omission, the good we didn't do. The good news is, near the end of our running the race of life, we can access, as never before, the grace and mercy of our Lord and Savior Jesus Christ.

We older folks can bear witness to the younger generations the reality of the person and work of Jesus Christ as our passing into God's presence draws near. We can face death with confidence, not in ourselves, but in His grace and mercy.

While we are here on earth, we should be engaged in this life, because if we're here on earth, we have a purpose yet to be lived out. We're compelled by the loving presence and working of Christ within us to serve him, right up until the end, whatever form that service might take, even with our growing limitations. "Christ's love compels us" is what the apostle Paul wrote in 2 Corinthians 5:14.

John Piper wrote, "So finishing life to the glory of Christ means using whatever strength and eyesight and hearing and mobility and resources we have left to treasure Christ and in that joy to serve people—that is, to seek to bring them with us into the everlasting enjoyment of Christ. Serving people, and not ourselves, as the overflow of treasuring Christ makes Christ look great."[30] Yes, we can make Christ look great by having him live through us even as the time of our passing draws near.

I quoted Psalm 92:14 in a previous day's reading because it was fitting. We conclude this day's reading with that verse and the addition of verse fifteen. Concerning God's people, the psalmist declared, "They will still bear fruit in old age, they will stay fresh and green, proclaiming, 'The Lord is upright; he is my Rock, and there is no wickedness in him'" (Psalm 92:14–15). Displaying Christ until the end— this is finishing well.

PERSEVERING TO THE END—DAY 28

Finishing well, the subject of yesterday's reading, can't happen unless we persevere to the end. Persevering means keeping on keeping on. This can be a challenge in our senior years. The relinquishing of responsibilities and duties means there's less external motivation for getting up and getting going each morning.

R. Paul Stevens wrote, "For many people, retirement is unorganized sloth. It could be argued that of all the seven deadlies, sloth is the one most present with the aging. They have no initiative, no passion, no deep interest to explore, no concern to continue to make a difference. So, they become couch potatoes in front of the television or, if they have the money, amuse themselves to death with one pleasure after another."[31]

During my years pastoring, I kept busy, using a pocket appointment calendar for keeping track of pastoral home visits, hospital calls, meetings, funerals, weddings, and more. I started serious work on next Sunday's message on Tuesday morning, working on the message each morning until Saturday when I committed my sermon to mind and heart for delivery before the people on Sunday. Yes, I had many external motivations prompting me to get up and get going every day—except Monday, usually my day off. Now that I'm retired from pastoral ministry, these external motivations are no long present. I must look deep within myself for a renewed and fresh call of the Lord to live each day for him.

Growing older gracefully means we keep growing into the person he wants us to be until the end, that we keep doing what the Lord has for us to do until the end. We are not yet all we can be until Christ calls us home and finishes perfecting us. We have not yet done all we can do until we enter his presence and hear him say, "Well done, good and faithful servant" (Matthew 25:21, 23)!

As the apostle Paul wrote in his later years, "Not that I have already obtained this or am already perfect, but I press on to make it my own, because Christ Jesus has made me his own. Brothers, I do not consider that I have made it my own. But one thing I do: forgetting what lies behind and straining forward to what lies ahead, I press on toward the goal for the prize of the upward call of God in Christ Jesus" (Philippians 3:12–14 ESV).

Sadly, as we grow older, we can imitate the life cycle of the sea squirt. The sea squirt starts out as a swimming larva, much like a tadpole. Then, it attaches to an object, settling into place. The larva's nervous system, including a tiny brain, dissolves, becoming the familiar looking sea squirt, a conglomeration of filter feeding cells. Let's not go the way of the sea squirt.

In some ways, as we move through our senior years, our world grows smaller. Relationships with previous coworkers and customers diminish as the postretirement years increase in number. We might not have the energy for maintaining an active lifestyle as we did in former years. If we compare ourselves to a river, we might say that our river of life isn't as wide as it was, but the good news is the river can go deeper.

Developing a new depth of living can be a fresh agenda for us. We have more time for reading, reflection, and relating than we did during the busy former years. Scoop up a jar of fast-moving muddy river water and observe what happens. Watch, as the water in the jar becomes still, the silt and other suspended materials settle to the bottom, and the water becomes clear. In the stillness that can come with being older, what had been continuously stirred about in busier years now has a chance to settle down, giving us greater clarity about what is important.

Giving up on living could be tempting as our get up and go has gotten up and gone. But the Lord calls us to keep going, in one way or another, until he calls us home to heaven.

The *Pain Medicine Journal* reported a study involving sixty-three people between the ages of sixty and eighty-seven concerning chronic pain and how they managed it. The study showed that "a major theme of perseverance emerged" with many of the participants commenting about the "need to go on."[32] Martin Luther King, Jr. is often credited with saying, "If you can't fly then run, if you can't run then walk, if you can't walk then crawl, but whatever you do you have to keep moving forward."

Perseverance is a trait we must continue applying, so we'll persevere to the end, otherwise we're not exhibiting perseverance. "You need to persevere so that when you have done the will of God, you will receive what he has promised" (Hebrews 10:36).

Walter Elliot, priest and missionary, is believed to have said, "Perseverance is not a long race; it is many short races one after the other." Endurance is only possible when we persevere one day at a time, one hour at a time, one minute at a time. What greater sense of accomplishment can there be than knowing we've persevered to the end.

Then we can say, as Paul wrote, "I have fought the good fight, I have finished the race, I have kept the faith. Now there is in store for me the crown of righteousness, which the Lord, the righteous Judge, will award to me on that day—and not only to me, but also to all who have longed for his appearing" (2 Timothy 4:7–8). Our last great accomplishment can be persevering to the end.

THE FINAL POLISHING OF LIFE—
DAY 29

People who polish stones use different abrasives placed in a turning drum with the stones. They start with a coarse abrasive, then several days later, switch to a finer abrasive, and days later to an even finer abrasive. Over several weeks, the rough stones tumbling in the turning drum with the abrasives become beautifully polished stones. We can also pick up smooth stones along a lakeshore that have been polished over countless years being buffeted in the waves and sand.

I keep a few polished stones around as a reminder that God wants to polish my life, taking off the rough edges, through that which buffets me about every day. When we've reached our senior years, we can think of different ways and different times we've faced abrasive situations in life: challenges, difficulties, problems, setbacks, and tragedies.

We might have retired from active work, but we haven't retired from facing those abrasive situations in life. In fact, the senior years bring their own fresh take on them.

As has often been said, growing old isn't for the faint of heart. In major ways, we're survivors, having arrived at the stage of life in which we now find ourselves. However, we could yet face our biggest challenges, including the statistical probability that death will claim family and friends around our own age, increasing health issues, and those conditions leading ultimately to our own death.

Our goals for the future are undoubtedly fewer, our bucket list edited down to a shorter list, but there is much yet for us that needs doing in these later years. These are the years when God is doing the final polishing. We remind people, PBPWMGINFWMY, Please Be Patient With Me, God Is Not Finished With Me Yet.

Ruth Graham, wife of evangelist Billy Graham, requested this epitaph be placed on her gravestone, inspired by a road construction sign she had seen, "End of Construction— Thank you for your patience." God has us under "construction" until the moment we die. Our sanctification process isn't over until the second he takes us to himself completing the sanctifying process instantaneously. The apostle Paul wrote, "Being confident of this, that he who began a good work in you will carry it on to completion until the day of Christ Jesus" (Philippians 1:6).

God is completing the polishing process in this last stage of our lives. As we age, we often find the usual things in life that kept us busy and entertained us shrink in importance. Growing older is a wonderful time for refocusing, reaffirming what's truly important—the all-surpassing worth of knowing Christ. John Piper wrote, "If we are going to make Christ look glorious in the last years of our lives, we must be satisfied in him. He must be our Treasure. And the life that we live must flow from this all-satisfying Christ."[33] As we grow into old age, we can commit to being weaned from the things of this world, developing a greater thirst and hunger for Christ.

There's direction and comfort in the lyrics of that old familiar hymn, "Turn Your Eyes Upon Jesus" by Helen Howarth Lemmel. The lyrics describe a soul that is weary and troubled and how the difficulties in this world dim when we turn our eyes of faith upon Jesus.

The unique abrasives added to the rotating drum of our life's experience as we're "turning" older (pun intended) are, indeed, intended to knock off our rough edges, polishing us up so we're more Christlike. This is neither a fun nor an easy process. We need the Lord's help in this final progression with polishing before he takes us home to his heaven. We do have God's promise of his help. Jude wrote that God "is able to keep you from stumbling and to present you before his glorious presence without fault and with great joy" (Jude 1:24).

As we grow older there's an increased risk of stumbling and falling. That could be true physically speaking but doesn't have to be true spiritually speaking. The Lord "is able to keep you from stumbling," as Jude told us. We can finish well.

Throughout the story of our lives, becoming more like Christ is our calling, but it often seems our greatest challenges for doing so come in living out the last chapters of our story here on earth. Believing our greatest growth is behind us is tempting. Life doesn't have to be this way and shouldn't be. We don't have to stumble in stepping out in faith into our later years. We can continue walking confidently, conforming more to Christ. We can continue being fruitful followers of his.

What do most plants do in their final stage of life, just before they wither and die? They produce their fruit. A plant spends most of its life sprouting, growing, growing some more, then flowering, which is usually considered the most beautiful stage. In the final stage, after flowering, it produces its fruit.

Spiritually, our senior years can be the most fruitful years of our life. Alice Fryling quoted Leighton Ford, "In this season, I can celebrate being more fruitful, even as I become less productive."[34]

In the final analysis, the fruitful Christian life is one which exhibits the fruit of the Spirit found in Galatians 5:22–23. "But the fruit of the Spirit is love, joy, peace, patience, kindness, goodness, faithfulness, gentleness, and self-control." God's final polishing in our senior years can result in us exhibiting this fruit as never before.

A TIME OF LETTING GO—DAY 30

Many of us find we've accumulated more stuff as we've moved through the years. Someone posted on Facebook, "When I was young, I was poor. But after years of hard work, I am no longer young." By God's grace, my wife and I can say we've never been poor, but neither have we been rich, at least by United States standards. Yet, over the years, we've managed to collect many possessions.

Downsizing is often a challenge we face as we move through our senior years. When we retired, moving from Michigan to Florida, we decided a lot of our stuff didn't have to move with us. We left some home furnishings for the folks who bought our Michigan house, gave some other items away, and burned a few things too.

A task I took on in dividing the domestic duties in our marriage was the weekly dusting. That's why, when we downsized, I encouraged dispensing with several shelves of knickknacks.

I have a train set given me over several Christmases by a couple in the church. The first year I was given the engine, track, and—I think—the caboose. Every year, they gave me another car or two for the train set. Each Christmas, I set up the track and train under our Christmas tree and enjoyed watching the cars journey around and around the Christmas tree. But several years ago, I bequeathed the train set to my son and his family. Now we go to their house at Christmastime, and I can enjoy the train there, going around and around their tree, without the work involved with setting it up or taking it down.

Yes, moving through the senior years might mean letting go of material things. We could also lose mobility (by giving up driving, for instance). The letting go of relationships through the attrition caused by death is often a stark reality. Then, too, there's the letting go of certain entertainment, hobbies, and other distractions. There's also the letting go of unfulfilled hopes and dreams.

I remember when we moved my father into a nursing home. His room was so small any guest had to pull out the folding chair leaning against the wall to have a seat. My father had been a farmer for many years, crisscrossing over a hundred and sixty acres of farmland, tending the crops and animals with tractors and a variety of farm machinery. Then my parents retired, moving into a modest house on a small lot in town. Now he occupied a tiny room in a nursing home. His possessions in that room were very few. My father's life, in space and possessions, kept shrinking.

This is a natural progression—this letting go—that shouldn't surprise us. The Roman statesman-philosopher Cicero said, "Can anything be more absurd in the traveler than to increase his luggage as he nears his journey's end?"

Christians have practiced many spiritual disciplines, including the discipline of simplicity. We who are moving through our senior years, can find ourselves practicing a variation of the spiritual discipline of simplicity by letting go of things, thus simplifying our lives. The writer of Ecclesiastes stated, "There is a time for everything, and a season for every activity under heaven ... a time to keep and a time to throw away" (Ecclesiastes 3:1, 6).

God intends letting go to be good for us. It's all part of his plan, as painful as that can be. Letting go gives us new clarity for what is important in life and what isn't so important. The best things in life can't be parked in a garage, put in the bank, or placed on a shelf. Philip Yancey quotes a scientist, who said, "Everything that can be counted does not necessarily count; everything that counts cannot necessarily be counted."[35]

The school of growing older teaches us the lesson that the accumulation and enjoyment of possessions is not most important. When the wealthy, powerful, and famous are asked what regrets they have, they will often respond they wish they had invested more time and effort in those near them. I can't recall anyone ever responding they wish they had spent less time with family and friends and more time making money and accumulating possessions.

What really counts are relationships, especially our relationship with God. John Piper wrote, "Knowing that we have an infinitely satisfying and everlasting inheritance in God just over the horizon of life makes us zealous in our few remaining years here to spend ourselves in the sacrifices of love, not the accumulation of comforts."[36]

We'll likely be saying goodbye to some with whom we're in a relationship, particularly many peers. This is part of the letting go. But we can also zealously invest in the relationships that are still available to us, the younger generations, our children, grandchildren, great-grandchildren, nieces and nephews, or others who have fewer years behind them. We can guard against ever having to say, "All my friends are gone." We should continually be making and nurturing younger friends. This way we always have people within our sphere of influence into whom we can pour ourselves.

Eventually, the aging process can isolate us from others. We can't get around like we did when visiting others. We might not be in good enough health to give attention to those who might want to visit us. Our world will quite likely keep growing smaller. There could come a time when we're usually alone. We're not alone, if we've cultivated a relationship with God. R. Paul Stevens wrote, "The reality is that aging involves progressive relinquishment until we have only one treasure left—Christ and the relationships we've made through him. Through the process we discover that aging is a spiritual discipline."[37]

Growing older is a time of letting go, but also a time when we can possess more fully that which is important and valuable.

THE BEST IS YET TO COME—DAY 31

I think it was around my fiftieth birthday when I faced the reality, very likely, my life was more than half over. Until then, I figured there were quite a few people who live into their nineties. At age forty-nine, I still thought there might be half of my life yet before me. I'd be ninety-eight but still under the hundred-year mark. If I kept eating bran muffins maybe I'd make it. But at age fifty, I had to admit I was over the hill, past the summit called the halfway point, and was on my way down toward the end.

Now I'm past seventy, more than twenty years later, and there's no denying the fact—the end is looming closer. People die at any age, but when we're in our senior years, we must face facts—statistically speaking, we don't have much time left.

As a pastor for nearly forty years, I presided at over three hundred and fifty funerals. In all those funeral messages, I proclaimed the hope of eternal life. I believed what I preached. After all, I was preaching truth from the Bible. As time goes by, and as I make my way through my senior years, this wonderful truth of eternal life has taken on greater personal relevance. I grasp the hope of eternal life more vigorously than ever.

Growing older gracefully can include a growing anticipation for the next phase of life, entry into God's presence
in his heaven. Throughout life, we often look forward to
the next stage. We looked forward to graduating from high
school, being an adult, landing a good job, getting married,
having children, seeing the children grow up and move out
on their own, enjoying grandchildren, and retiring. That's
where the looking forward often ends. Retirement should
not be the end of looking forward.

When we embrace a relationship with God through his
Son Jesus Christ, that relationship is forever. When God
reaches out to rescue us through the saving work his Son
Jesus offers, and we accept that grasp of his grace, he has
us in an eternal grip. This should result in a paradigm shift
in how we view death. Death should no longer be seen as
the end, but just a transition, a new beginning.

At several funerals I've conducted over the years, I
shared my parable of the unborn child leaving the world of
the womb, entering a new world. I share a variation here.

> Imagine twins in the womb who can think, wonder,
> hope, and doubt. What would they say to each other
> as they sensed their nine months of life in the womb
> coming to an end?
>
> "This life is getting uncomfortable, crowded," Baby 1 said.
>
> "I know," Baby 2 said. "It feels like we're leaving here
> soon, I feel the world pushing us out."
>
> "If we're leaving this world, then what?"
>
> "Maybe nothing. Maybe this is all there is."
>
> "But I think there's more than what we now have. I sense
> something beyond our world. There's the rhythm of
> another heart, and a soft voice, a calming, joyful voice, I
> think I hear. Then too, there's a sense we are being patted
> and soothingly massaged by something or someone."

Baby 2 reached out his hand through the embryonic fluid, touching Baby 1. "I know. I sense it too. But can it really be?"

"We love each other, but is there anyone beyond this world that would love us, or that we could love?"

"I don't know, it's hard imagining any existence other than this one," Baby 2 said.

"I feel something happening. I'm being squeezed from all sides. I think I must leave here."

"I don't want you to leave!"

"I can't help it! Am I dying?"

Baby 2 was silent for a few moments, then said, trying to be reassuring, "I think it will be okay, I'm feeling the squeezing now too. I believe we're going to another world. I'll be right behind you."

"So, you don't think we're dying?"

"No, I don't think so. I think it's something else," Baby 2 answered, then added, "See you on the other side."

"Yes, see you on the other side," Baby 1 replied as Baby 2 felt him leave.

Within a half hour, both Baby 1 and Baby 2 were nestled in the arms of their mother. Having had their first taste of their mother's milk, they now slept contentedly. It was heavenly.

Beyond the world of the womb is the warm, loving welcome experienced in a mother's arms. For the first time, the child can see the mother's smiling face and hear her voice distinctly. There will be warm milk and soft lullabies. A whole new amazing life begins, life very different from life in the world of the womb. What the unborn child would call death, we on this side of the process call birth.

We often hear the statement, "Getting older isn't so bad when you consider the alternative." I disagree. For the person in relationship with Christ, the alternative is much better. Yes, we have a God-given instinct to survive, trying to stay alive in this world. This instinct is what makes us hesitate to step out into the street when traffic's coming or jump off high places. Still, as we move through our senior years, realizing our time on earth is limited, we can be intentional about changing our perspective on dying and death.

We can do no better than adopting the attitude the apostle Paul had when writing the Philippians, "But our citizenship is in heaven. And we eagerly await a Savior from there, the Lord Jesus Christ, who, by the power that enables him to bring everything under his control, will transform our lowly bodies so that they will be like his glorious body" (Philippians 3:20–21).

Like Paul, we can eagerly await our Savior Jesus transferring our citizenship to heaven. Hope can permeate our minds, filling our hearts as we make our way through the senior years. We're not coming to the end of our life, but drawing closer to being born into an unimaginably wonderful new phase of our life with glorified new bodies inhabiting God's glorious heaven with him. The best is yet to come.

CONCLUSION

Thanks for joining me on this journey. The author/reader relationship tends to be one way—the author writes and the reader reads. However, I invite you to turn our journey into a two-way communication. I'd be delighted to hear from you. I'm sure you have some thoughts about what I've shared in these thirty-one reflections. I'd like to know what you think.

You might also have your own story or illustration concerning a subject we've covered. I invite you to email me at djclaassen@gmail.com and share your thoughts. Our journey together can continue.

We don't have to be like that old grump in Readlyn, Iowa, who I mentioned at the beginning of this small volume. We *can* grow older gracefully, finishing our journey well.

ABOUT THE AUTHOR

DAVID CLAASSEN is a retired pastor and author of several books. He and his wife, Diann, have been married over fifty years and are enjoying their retirement by dividing their time between a home in Florida to be near their son and his family and a home in Mexico to be near their daughter and her family. Relating to their grandchildren is their primary calling from God at this stage of their lives.

ENDNOTES

Day 3

1. Parker Palmer, *On the Brink of Everything* (Oakland: Berrett-Koehler, 2018), Kindle.

Day 5

2. Marilyn McEntyre, *A Faithful Farewell: Living Your Last Chapter with Love* (Grand Rapids: Wm. B. Eerdmans Publishing Co., 2015), Kindle.

Day 6

3. Palmer, *On the Brink of Everything*, Kindle.

Day 8

4. Calvin Miller, *Life Is Mostly Edges* (Nashville: Thomas Nelson, 2010), 373.

Day 9

5. John Newton, *The Letters of John Newton* (West Linn, OR: Monergism Books, 2010), p 937.

Day 13

6. Parker Palmer, "The Gift of Presence and the Perils of Advice," DailyGood.Org, (January 01, 2019), https://www.dailygood.org/story/2152/the-gift-of-presence-and-the-per-

ils-of-advice-parker-j-palmer/

7. Jocelyn Soriano, "The Gift of Your Presence," I Take Off the Mask, (September 16, 2014), https://itakeoffthe-mask.com/words-of-wisdom/gift-presence/

Day 14

8. Os Guiness, *The Call* (Nashville: Thomas Nelson, 2003), 180.

Day 15

9. Newton, *The Letters of John Newton*, loc. 15023.

Day 16

10. Wayne Grudem, *Systematic Theology: An Introduction to Biblical Doctrine* (Grand Rapids: Zondervan Academic, 1994), Kindle.

11. Philip Yancey, *Vanishing Grace* (Grand Rapids: Zondervan, 2014), 43.

12. Yancey, *Vanishing Grace*, 79.

Day 18

13. Timothy Keller, *Prayer: Experiencing Awe and Intimacy with God* (New York: Viking, 2014), 151.

Day 19

14. Frederick Buechner, *Secrets in the Dark: A Life in Sermons* (New York: HarperCollins, 2006), Kindle.

Day 20

15. Yancey, *Vanishing Grace*, 61.

Day 22

16. R. Paul Stevens, *Aging Matters: Finding Your Calling for the Rest of Your Life*, (Grand Rapids: Wm. B. Eerdmans Publishing Company, 2016), Kindle.

17. Timothy Keller, *The Freedom of Self-Forgetfulness* (Lancashire, UK: 10 Publishing, 2012), Kindle.

18. Newton, *The Letters of John Newton*, loc. 19710.

19. Keller, *Self-Forgetfulness*, Kindle.

20. Keller, *Self-Forgetfulness*, Kindle.

Day 24

21. McEntyre, *A Faithful Farewell*, Kindle.

22. Stevens, *Aging Matters*, Kindle.

23. *Matthew Henry Commentary on the Whole Bible*, biblestudytools.com, https://www.biblestudytools.com/commentaries/matthew-henry-concise/jeremiah/29.html.

24. Charles Cummings, *The Mystery of the Ordinary*, (New York: Harper Collins Publishers, 1982), Preface.

Day 25

25. McEntyre, *A Faithful Farewell*, Kindle.

Day 26

26. John Piper, *Rethinking Retirement: Finishing Life for the Glory of Christ* (Wheaton: Crossway Books, 2008), 29.

27. Stevens, *Aging Matters*, e-book 18.

28. Stevens, *Aging Matters*, Kindle.

29. Stevens, *Aging Matters*, Kindle.

Day 27

30. Piper, *Rethinking Retirement*, 9.

Day 28

31. Stevens, *Aging Matters,* Kindle.

32. Beatrice Sofaer-Bennett, etal., "Perseverance by Older People in Their Management of Chronic Pain: A Qualitative Study," *Pain Medicine* 8, no. 3 (April 2007): 271–280, https://doi.org/10.1111/j.1526-4637.2007.00297.x.

Day 29

33. Piper, *Rethinking Retirement,* 18.

34. Alice Fryling, *Aging Faithfully: The Holy Invitation of*

Growing Older (Carol Stream: NavPress, 2021), 9.

Day 30

35. Yancey, *Vanishing Grace*, 159.

36. Piper, *Rethinking Retirement*, 6.

37. Stevens, *Aging Matters*, Kindle.

www.ingramcontent.com/pod-product-compliance
Lightning Source LLC
Chambersburg PA
CBHW071755090426
42737CB00012B/1824